NOW IS THE TIME

Paul Rowntree Clifford

NOW IS THE TIME

Changing Church Structures

COLLINS

St James's Place, London, 1970

SBN 00 215556 7

Printed in Great Britain by
Collins Clear-Type Press
London & Glasgow

Contents

Preface

As the title implies, this book is written out of a sense of urgency. It is evident to the most casual observer that the Christian Church everywhere is facing a major crisis in adapting itself to the rapidly changing world of today. My conviction is that it has not an indefinite period of time in which to do it, but that decisions of crucial importance must be taken now. The danger is that much too little will be done, much too slowly and much too late.

On the other hand, the need for renewal is more widely recognized than ever before, evidenced by the fact that it has been the theme of almost every major conference of Christians since the Second Vatican Council. Pope John XXIII, whose elevation to the See of Rome was at first supposed to be an interim measure, unexpectedly announced that the time had come for radical change in the Church's understanding of its mission. In the event, his conviction that the hour had come for momentous reforms was confirmed by the overwhelming response from Roman Catholics all over the world. It was as if the lid had been taken off a seething cauldron, and Pope John's declared purpose of bringing the Church up to date was widely recognized as the beginning of an answer to all those who were increasingly conscious of being imprisoned within a rigid ecclesiastical framework.

The Italian word *aggiornamento*, which has the double

connotation of modernizing and renewal, soon became current coin beyond the bounds of the Roman Church. The Fourth Assembly of the World Council of Churches at Uppsala took as its theme 'Behold I make all things new', and the Tenth Lambeth Conference, which met immediately afterwards, continued the same keynote with 'The Renewal of the Church in Faith, Ministry and Unity'. But as we begin to assess the concrete results of all this thinking and talking, we are bound to ask whether they will add up to anything in terms of action. When all the conferences have ended, will there be any real change? Or will the Church remain much the same, settling for the *status quo*, cloaked by a mountain of words and tons of paper? 'Words, words, words; I'm sick of words', cried Eliza Doolittle in *My Fair Lady*. 'Sing me no song; read me no rhyme; don't waste my time. Show me!' The Church cannot escape this challenge from within and without the ranks of its membership. Words are no substitute for action.

The fear that in the end there would be no radical changes was strongly voiced at Uppsala, particularly by the youth participants, and the encyclicals of Pope Paul VI on doctrine and on family planning have merely underlined for a host of people the deeply felt suspicion that conservative influences are bound ultimately to prevail. But we simply dare not settle for such a conclusion. If radical changes do not take place, and take place within the next decade, the Church will be condemned to irrelevance for most of the rising generation, and for many older men and women too. The signs are plain to be seen. The decline in open church membership and in the number of candidates for ordination, resignations from the ministry and widespread disillusionment with organized religion, all add up to a state of affairs that cannot be brushed under the carpet.

In the face of all this there are some, perhaps an alarmingly growing number, who see no hope of reform or renewal within the existing ecclesiastical structures, and advocate a new start, abandoning the Church as it is now constituted. This is a view I cannot share. For one thing it represents an attempt to break with the historical past, which is a major weakness of all contemporary radicalism. We shall fall into the most grievous error if we equate renewal with accommodation to the transient patterns of life and thought which represent the mood of the moment. There is a wisdom of the ages, the wisdom of what a former colleague of mine described as the antique world, the world that persists through change, acquiring and exhibiting indestructible value through its very persistence, which we ignore at our peril. What is more, the Church's continuity down the centuries, its unbroken link with the saints of every generation, is part and parcel of its priceless heritage. A Church that began *de novo* in the twentieth century would not only be grievously impoverished; it would scarcely be the Church at all. Whatever the difficulties, we must begin with the Church as it is, taking care to preserve all that is of enduring value from the past, cherishing its continuity through the ages, and yet prepared for the most radical renewal of that which we have inherited. We must reject the iconoclasm which would discount both past and present in the supposed interests of the future. At the same time we must be prepared to have all things made new, transformed but not abandoned.

Nevertheless, if we are to avoid the extreme counsel of despair, we have to give full weight to the reasons which induce some of our fellow-Christians to be inclined in that direction. We dare not continue pedalling along with things as they are, fearful of radical change lest those who are set in their ways will be unduly disturbed. Nor may we postpone the hour of decision, waiting for the Church at large to catch up with the twentieth century. Events are moving too rapidly for that; they are succeeding one another at breakneck speed. Indeed, one of the major characteristics of the present age, distinguishing it most sharply from the epochs preceding it, is the tempo of change in which we are all engulfed. The Church is not accustomed to think in these terms, and so is in grave danger of being left in a backwater. To quote the famous words of Shakespeare:

> There is a tide in the affairs of men,
> Which, taken at the flood, leads on to fortune;
> Omitted, all the voyage of their life
> Is bound in shallows and in miseries.

The Church does find itself in the shallows today, and there it will stick while the world rushes by unless a new sense of urgency fires Christian leaders and captures the imagination of the rank and file. The moment for far-reaching decisions does not lie ten, twenty or a hundred years ahead. Now is the time.

Some readers may feel impatient with the sequence of the argument as it stands, because it deals with the reform of church structures before coming to grips with the crisis of faith which confronts us everywhere. If so they should read the last chapter first; for it is really the lynch-pin of the whole book. Radicals may find it too orthodox for their liking, in so far as they expect the far-reaching proposals of earlier chapters to be reflected in a revolutionary recasting of the Faith. But I must say what I believe, and I have chosen to interpret the word 'radical' in this connexion as 'digging to the roots' rather than as alignment with the critical left wing in theology.

My thanks are due to Dr Norman Goodall and Professor Eric Fenn who have been kind enough to read the whole typescript and have made a number of helpful suggestions, and to the Rev. Ian Ross, the theological colleges' secretary of the Student Christian Movement, who gave me the benefit of his careful criticism of the chapter on the ministry. I am also greatly indebted to Miss Frances Williams who typed and retyped the manuscript and prepared it for publication.

PAUL R. CLIFFORD
Selly Oak Colleges
Birmingham

July 1969

Chapter One

The Church Incarnate

When Dr Visser 't Hooft was interviewed on television soon after his retirement from the General Secretaryship of the World Council of Churches, he was asked what he thought was the major challenge facing the Christian Church today. He replied that above everything else the real Church was called to break through the structures it had inherited from the past and in which it is now imprisoned. More negatively, the same conviction was voiced by Charles Davis in his explanation of why he felt compelled to leave the Roman Church. He said that he had been forced to the conclusion that the Church of his upbringing places authority above the love of truth and as an institution actually militates against a genuine concern for people and their ultimate welfare: they are too often its victims; and he added that, as far as he could tell, this is the case with all the other denominations too. Here is an indictment of the first magnitude which has to be treated with the fullest possible seriousness.

In the face of such a challenge it is not enough to talk about changes in the ecclesiastical structures—reunion schemes and plans for reorganization—important as they are. Nothing less than a fundamental change of outlook is required; for without this there will be no real incentive to alter anything at all. That is where we must begin.

At once we are compelled to recognize that the Gospel

dictates an attitude to all questions which it is extremely difficult for human beings to adopt. The Christian Faith is centred in the doctrine of the Incarnation: the conviction that 'the Word became flesh and dwelt among us'.[1] This means that the Church is founded on the belief that God has identified himself with man in the depths of his predicament. He has become incarnated in the world as it is, and the entire life of Jesus is a demonstration of that fact.

It is scarcely possible to exaggerate the contrast between this identification of God with the world of his creation and popular ideas of the way in which he is related to it. Instinctively we think of omnipotence in terms of man's exercise of power, imagining God as a magnified Oriental potentate, enthroned above the world and controlling the course of events. That was not the way in which Jesus conceived his role as embodying the will of his Father. He chose a road which ultimately led to Golgotha. As a famous Methodist minister once said, 'If Jesus Christ is God, he does not behave as one who is on top of things. If I were on top, I would look round for a throne on which to sit. He accepted a cross whereon to hang. When I am on top, I think of my rights. He was concerned with his burden.'[2] Admittedly he was Master and Lord, but this was paradoxically expressed in adopting the role of a servant, 'being born in the likeness of men',[3] and identified with them in all their frailty.

Now it has to be acknowledged that in the main the Church has singularly failed to reflect the servant image or to convince ordinary people of being genuinely identified with them. It has adopted a magisterial role, standing aloof from the world, and proclaiming that men and women had to turn to it for salvation. When it has not been pronouncing judgement on the sins of the flesh and the social order or telling people what they ought to believe, its characteristic message has been an invitation to come within its institutional structure in order to find forgiveness of sin, reconciliation with God and spiritual regeneration. 'Come to church' is an appeal that has been heard all too often, placarded on notice boards and broadcast from pulpits. When I try to put myself in the shoes of those who pass by our ecclesiastical buildings and see the way we advertise ourselves, I find myself asking 'Why on earth should anyone be expected to respond to this kind of invitation?' If I were not already committed, wild horses would not drag me up those high steps and through those stiff doors. The evangelist's appeal, 'Come to Christ', is not much better; for it carries with it the suggestion that our Lord and his representatives stand on an ecclesiastical platform above the common herd and can only be reached by climbing out of the mire.

The approach of Jesus was quite different. For him going took precedence over coming. He had been heralded by 'a man sent from God, whose name was John'[4] and he himself was profoundly convinced of being sent into the world by the Father. Certainly he gave the invitation, 'Come to me, all whose work is hard, whose load is heavy; and I will give you relief.'[5] *But that invitation was given from within the context of involvement.* It was not uttered from a pedestal or a throne, but from the place he had chosen among the humble men and women of his day, even among the prostitutes, the sharp business operators and those who seemed bent on pursuing the transitory pleasures of life. Jesus was to be found amongst those who were facing disease, loneliness and despair, amongst those who were trying to grapple with the problems of everyday existence and so often failing in the attempt. He was there in the midst of people who were laughing, sometimes cynically and sometimes light-heartedly, as well as in the midst of those for whom the burden of living had become almost intolerable. He was identified with ordinary folk of all kinds and ended up crucified between two thieves. This was the context of his invitation. He said 'Come' to those to whom he had really come himself.

The religious leaders of the day were scandalized. They were horrified that anyone claiming to represent God should keep such doubtful company. This was not the way in which they understood God's relationship to men. Theirs was a magisterial conception of religion and their inward security was threatened by the Rabbi from Nazareth. He was turning organized religion upside down, and they had either to reject him altogether or radically alter their whole approach. Of course it was easier to preserve the magisterial role; for to follow Jesus was to become exposed, and that was both uncomfortable and dangerous.

The Pharisees were not bad men. In the main they were deeply sincere and prepared to make great sacrifices for their beliefs. The trouble was that their attitude was wrong: they misread the will of God, and in their fear of being contaminated by the world and losing their authority, they adopted a stance which distorted all that was best in the Jewish heritage. The Church has fallen into the same kind of trap, and for much the same reasons. What is needed for renewal is a change of basic approach: a realistic appreciation of the Christian mission as total involvement, even to the point of witnessing to the presence of God in the world outside the ecclesiastical structures. The point is put with persuasive force by Monica Furlong in introducing her trenchant indictment of the Church of which she is a member:

> I do not wish to discuss the administrative changes, the redeployment of the clergy, the new or rediscovered liturgical practices, disestablishment, ecumenicalism, or any of the other reforms which are either being enacted or else are under discussion. Profound as such reforms may be in their effect, they are of less importance than the large change of heart and mind of which they are the outward form. If the change took place, then many of the reforms might occur anyway. If it doesn't take place, it won't matter whether they happen or not.[6]

What sort of transformation in attitude is required if the Church is to be seen as the Church of the Incarnation? The answer, I believe, lies along three lines: genuine identification with men and women in their quest for truth, in their moral struggles and in the depths of their emotional life.

First of all, Christians must be clearly identified with those who are concerned to know the truth, whatever it may be. This will entail the frank admission of our ignorance about many things, our doubts and bewilderment about others, and our partial insight right across the board. Instead of proclaiming to an unbelieving world that the Church has got all the answers, with the implication that they are neatly tied up in parcels ready for immediate delivery, Christians have to admit that there are many things they don't know and that those they have begun to grasp are imperfectly understood and are capable of only inadequate expression.

This implies coming to grips with the widespread confusion that prevails as to the nature of truth in general and

Christian truth in particular. Most people seem to suppose that truth is a perfectly simple concept which everybody understands: whatever we say or think which exactly corresponds to things as they actually are is true; whatever does not is false. But such an assumption conceals serious difficulties about the relation of language and concepts to the world of reality. In particular, it glosses over a basic distinction which has to be drawn if we are to achieve any clarity of understanding. Broadly speaking, there are two quite different senses in which the word 'true' is used. The first relates to our own thoughts about the nature of things and the manner in which we give expression to them. We may call this 'subjective truth': the validity (or otherwise) of our conceiving and articulating what is presented to our minds. On the other hand, we may speak of 'objective truth' as the reality with which we are confronted, including the reality of ourselves, which is not of our formulating and which always exceeds our capacity to comprehend. It is in this sense of the word that St John's Gospel records the claim 'I am . . . the Truth'.[7] Clearly there is no idea here of the truth of a concept or a proposition. The claim being made is that reality is to be found embodied in the person of Jesus of Nazareth. To assert that something is there to be comprehended and expressed is one thing; to comprehend and express what this means is another. In so far as this distinction is valid, the sheer givenness of reality is the touchstone by which the adequacy of our subjective truth is to be judged.

Now I believe that we have to admit that all subjective truth is provisional and never an exhaustive exposure of the nature of things as they are. This applies to everything, from what we say about ordinary objects in the world around us to the assertions we make about God. Our limitations are such that we are incapable of complete comprehension, however much we may feel that this is an affront to our pride. We are all tempted to claim far more for our capacities than is warranted, and this is particularly so in an age when man is conquering nature to an extent that would have been beyond the wildest imagination of our forefathers. Success is going to our heads, and we need to be cut down to size, to be reminded that we are subject to a world of reality which lets us into some of its secrets but eludes our grasp at the same time. This does not mean that there are some things which we can fully comprehend while others are hidden from us. If that were so we could confidently look to a gradual, or perhaps even rapid, extension of the field of knowledge until mystery was banished from the universe altogether and man could at last stand on an Olympian height, master of all he surveyed. That is sheer delusion. Our grasp of everything is partial; we see all things as 'puzzling reflections in a mirror',[8] with the result that all our truth is provisional.

This is not to imply that what we say is inevitably untrue but that subjective truth, our truth, is a matter of degree. It is a case of fitting our thought and language to the incalculable richness of reality, recognizing that our concepts and the expression of them are always inadequate, and being prepared to discard them when they are replaceable by more appropriate forms. The relation of thought and language to that which they designate is one of the great unsolved problems in philosophy. However, enough has been written on the subject to put us on our guard against adopting any oversimplified solution. The common assumption that for anything to be true there must be an exact one-to-one correspondence between 'the facts' and our thought and speech about them ignores the difference between concepts and language on the one hand and the givenness of reality on the other, as well as failing to attach due weight to the admittedly provisional character of so much that we try to say. If it is the analogy of a photograph that we have in mind, we have only to remind ourselves that a photograph is not the equivalent of its subject.[9] While the picture of my mother reminds me of someone I knew and loved, it does not embody the real person.

Perhaps we can go no further than to say that all our thought and language points to a world of reality immeasurably richer in content than any of our forms of comprehension and expression can exhaust. The latter are like signposts or maps telling us something we want to know without pretending to be adequate substitutes for the place or territories to which they refer. For example, we recognize that all the guide books, maps, photographs and paintings of the Lake District could not possibly expose the full beauty of that lovely part of England. We have to see it for ourselves, and when we do see it, it transcends our capacity to formulate in thought or words. By so much more are we cut down to size in face of the mysteries of religion. We dare not claim that we can comprehend the divine nature or exhaust the depths of God's revelation of himself to man. At best we bear testimony to that which we have begun to see, acknowledging that all creeds and confessions are but halting and inadequate attempts to express the truth that shatters our framework of thinking and speaking.

This conclusion is likely to be deeply disturbing to a good many people who will object that, if it is accepted, Christians are condemned to a morass of relativity with no authoritative gospel for themselves or for anyone else. While this is almost certain to be the reaction of biblical and ecclesiastical conservatives, it will by no means be confined to them alone. Many of those who would dissociate themselves from any extreme position still believe that there must be certain formulae to which the Church is finally committed. This is a sort of crypto-fundamentalism resulting in a great deal of confused thinking. On the contrary, the fear of relativism rests upon a failure to grasp the fact that objectivity is not safeguarded in human language. It is simply not the case, as many seem to suppose, that we are faced with only two possible alternatives: either the absolute finality of our verbal definitions or sheer agnosticism in which we are committed to nothing. There is a third position which delivers us from pure subjectivism as well as from what is really irreverent dogmatism: we may hold firmly to the givenness of the Gospel in the activity of God without claiming finality for man's comprehension of it or his way of expressing that comprehension.

The approach for which I am contending can be clarified by considering the function of the great creeds of Christendom. In essence they are abstracts of Christian belief, statements in the most summary form of the Faith to which the Church is committed. In no sense do they pretend to be exhaustive exposures of that to which they refer. This is underlined by the very word the early fathers used to designate them—the Latin *symbolum*, from which we derive our 'symbol', originally denoting a sign pointing beyond itself to something else. Moreover, it has frequently been observed that the ancient creeds are more explicit in what they exclude than in what they assert. They were designed to counteract heresies, so labelled because the councils of the Church were persuaded that these rejected formulae represented one-sided and misleading attempts to crystallize the essence of the Faith. But the declarations on which agreement was ultimately reached were themselves open-ended, presenting a challenge to interpretation which has led to the production of a mountain of books over the centuries.

The same kind of thing can be said about the Bible. Indeed, both the Bible and the creeds bear witness to the divine revelation without fully exposing it or exhausting it. If we suppose it possible to equate human words with the divine Word, we fall into cardinal error. The divine Word reaches us through human words, but that is a very different matter from presuming we have God imprisoned within human language. That is why the notions of inerrancy and infallibility as applied either to Holy Scripture or ecclesiastical formulae have to be rejected as attempts to get God within our control.

Doubtless this will provoke the rejoinder that I have entirely missed the point. The contention of both biblical and ecclesiastical conservatives is not that man has to be in a position to control the truth, but that God himself has imparted his revelation in words that are absolute and final; they are not ordinary human words, but words that are raised on to another plane altogether by the express decree of God. They have the divine *imprimatur* upon them, and therefore it is for us to submit to their authority. It would be blasphemous for man to claim to master God through human language, but the roles are reversed once we recognize that God has chosen to disclose himself in this way.

Those who argue thus do not seem to have faced the real difficulties inherent in their position. What are the grounds for assuming that God commits himself to inerrant and therefore final verbal formulae? There is nothing in the Bible to suggest this. On the contrary, the *prima facie* evidence is all against it. If it were the case, as some biblical conservatives maintain, that God guaranteed not only the content of the Scriptures but also the words in which it is expressed, why should there be so many inconsistencies and discrepancies which the proponents of this particular theory have to explain away by the exercise of the most tortuous ingenuity? And the same forced interpretation is applied to what are regarded as questions of substance. In short, a doctrine of inerrancy or infallibility, whether of the contents or words of Scripture, would, as John Oman once said, 'disturbingly suggest the scandal of God's negligence, casting doubt not merely on his power but on his efficiency'.[10] The *prima facie* evidence is all against such a view of the Bible, and this conclusion is overwhelmingly supported by a century of patient and careful analysis of the documents by a host of notable scholars.

The fact is that those who bear testimony in the Scriptures to God's mighty acts show all the signs of human limitations. Is not the Old Testament the record of those to whom and through whom the divine purpose was gradually unfolded in spite of the all too human perspective that characterized them even at their best? Were not the disciples of Jesus rebuked on more than one occasion for their partial and sometimes distorted understanding of their master? The constant theme of the Scriptures is human fallibility in comprehending the divine revelation, and that has to be our starting point if we are to take the Bible seriously. We are not entitled to presuppose an inerrancy and a finality which the Bible itself contradicts.

The reason for insisting on propositional infallibility, whether of Scripture or creed, is patently psychological: the desire for security on human terms. Surely one of the strangest anomalies in this position is the supposition of its adherents that they are standing for the objectivity of the Gospel. In reality theirs is the most palpable form of subjectivism: the insistence that unless man has the measure of truth, truth itself is lost. So far from the denial of the inerrancy and finality of propositional statements being the unwarranted subjectivism of bringing human criticism to bear on the revelation of God, it is the refusal to impose on the divine revelation criteria derived from human prejudice. In contrast, I am claiming that we need to recognize ourselves as subject to what we cannot delimit; and on this basis the whole Bible and the creeds are to be held provisionally true in the sense that they bear testimony to the ultimate truth, while they are at the same time open-ended, pointing beyond themselves to the inexhaustible wealth of the grace of God.

Unequivocal adoption of this approach would liberate the Church from its authoritarianism without letting go its anchorage in the givenness of the Gospel. It would mean Christians coming out into the open and admitting the finitude they share with everybody else and the limitations of their knowledge over against the unimaginable richness of the truth by which they live but which is ever beyond their full comprehension. Perhaps the most difficult thing for the organized Church to do is to forsake its magisterial role in relation to the truth and become the learning Church. If it is arguable that within the realm of education generally we do not need more teachers, but more learners who will explore the world of knowledge with their pupils, the very word 'disciple' in Christian usage by that much more implies an openness to God and his revelation of himself in Christ which ill accords with a confident declaration that Christians are masters of the truth. The Church needs to be seen as reverent before the truth, identified with all those who recognize that they are not omniscient, but who, as philosophers, scientists, artists, men of letters or ordinary folk endowed with natural curiosity, are prepared with all the honesty and integrity they can summon to follow the light that is given to them. If that were so, then instead of being accused of setting ecclesiastical authority above the love of truth, the Church would be seen as incarnated amongst men in the quest for understanding, in the vanguard of those who recognize the folly of extravagant human pretensions.

In the second place, the Church must be identified with man in his moral predicament. This means really understanding what that moral predicament is. Too often it is thought of simply in terms of outward conduct: what ought I to do in a given situation: what line of action should be pursued in order to achieve social justice, racial harmony and international peace. In the inter-personal realm the Christian standard has been broadly based on the Ten Commandments: respect the life and property of others, tell the truth, be sexually chaste, look to your neighbour's welfare, honour God and keep one day in the week sacred to him, though unfortunately all of this has frequently been couched in negative rather than positive terms. For the most part it has been virtually taken for granted that such a standard of conduct would seem obviously reasonable to any normal person. As for social and international affairs, the general principles have appeared to be self-evident for Christian and non-Christian alike, though there has been and still is widespread disagreement about the steps which need to be taken to put them into effect.

While there has been a considerable consensus of agreement, at least in the West, regarding these standards, there are obvious signs that for increasing numbers of people they are regarded either as inadequate or as much too formal. They do not seem to make contact with the deep currents in human personality which are so often submerged under a cover of respectability or else break out in violent kinds of expression. The fact is that the basic moral questions are not about what men and women should *do* but about what they should *be*, not about what specific policies should be pursued, but about the nature of society as such. This is, of course, elementary to anyone who takes the New Testament seriously or has thought about the Christian understanding of man and society. But it is more than doubtful whether Christian thinking has come to grips with the actual predicament of the majority of ordinary people in a way that they can recognize or appreciate. Even when the magisterial stance is forsaken and we begin to talk about being on common ground in sharing the same sinful condition, even when we say that all men from Pope and Archbishop to prisoner in the dock and outcast on 'skid row' stand alike under the judgement of God and in need of his grace, is there any real mutual understanding? Have we got behind the theological language to the experienced reality of the human predicament?

We have not far to look for where this is being exposed today. Many modern novelists are doing it, uncovering and interpreting the agonizing struggle of man to find his identity and relate himself significantly to other people. A vivid example is the much publicized work of the American writer, Philip Roth, whose most recent book, *Portnoy's Complaint*, is estimated to have netted close on a million dollars even prior to issue. Its hero is an Assistant Commissioner of Human Opportunity in the city of New York: an apparently ordinary public servant, enjoying a successful career and exemplifying the ideals of the Kennedy era. But the author portrays him as a totally different person when lying on the psychologist's couch. All the pent-up feelings of frustration, guilt and fear pour out in a torrent of words, revealing the tension of living at two levels. The sketch of Alexander Portnoy is held to be that of a typical American, conforming in public to accepted standards of respectability but inwardly ruled by uncontrolled passions. There is no way to reconcile the one with the other, and the result is moral schizophrenia.

On the whole Americans are perhaps more self-analytical than most other Westerners, but there can be no doubt that the tension between overt standards of conduct and the urges of the inner life, which frequently erupt in destructive behaviour, is endemic to human nature. Eroticism, desire for sensual excitement of all kinds, acquisitiveness, thirst for power over other people and a tendency to violence in speech if not in action are not far beneath the surface of every human life. Often they are held in check by the conventions of society and accepted codes of conduct. Sometimes they take command in defiant anti-social behaviour. Nowadays we are witnessing the phenomenon of their open exploitation in the name of the free expression of personality.

Alongside these inward urges, which are the dominant theme of the contemporary novel, stage and screen, are the qualities of generosity, kindliness, compassion and self-sacrifice, all too often underestimated and underplayed by the sophisticated exponents of modern culture. Sometimes these qualities come to the surface in the most unlikely individuals who seem to have allowed full rein to their destructive passions. Most people, however, are conscious, in so far as they reflect at all, that these are dispositions which should be cultivated, even if they are submerged by sensuousness and self-regard. But however different we human beings may be from one another, whether we are torn apart by our passions and aspirations, or live with a precarious inward armistice, or wrestle with conflict, the root of our moral predicament lies here: in the inner springs of life of which overt conduct is sometimes the natural fruit, but sometimes the misleading expression. If the Church is to be really identified with ordinary men and women, if it is to be truly incarnated, this is the common ground: not in proclaiming from a pedestal a prepackaged code of outward behaviour, but in sympathetic awareness of the tensions and turmoil of man's inner life.

That is where the New Testament starts: with what man should *be* rather than with what he should *do*. This is not to say that what he does is unimportant. Far from it. But the Bible as a whole insists that action is grounded in the depths of human character and that this is distinctively formed in relationship with God. 'The fruit of the Spirit is love, joy, peace, patience, kindness, goodness, faithfulness, gentleness, self-control; against such there is no law.'[11] These dispositions cannot be legislated or codified in terms of outward conduct; they are the well-spring from which Christian conduct arises. Hence, for St Paul, faith is prior to works because a man needs to be open to divine influence if he is to be the sort of person who can act in a fully Christian way. It is only when a man is prepared to forsake reliance upon his own ability to become what he ought to be by doing what he thinks to be right that a distinctively Christian life is possible; and this is where modern man's real moral predicament is met—at the very depths of his life.

In maintaining such a position, St Paul is not radically departing from his Jewish heritage, still less from the teaching of Jesus. It is often forgotten that the prophetic tradition of Israel grounded obedience to the law in a right relationship with God and it was only in later Judaism that the attempt to cover every practical contingency led to the detailed elaboration of a code of conduct which obscured the fundamental importance of man's inner life. That is why Jesus came into conflict with the Pharisees. He was not minimizing the need for outward behaviour in conformity with the divine will. On the contrary, that was one of his recurring themes.[12] But he took issue with those who appeared content to stop there and who failed to recognize the place of dispositions and motives in assessing the morality of human action. 'What comes out of the mouth proceeds from the heart, and this defiles a man.'[13] St Paul was simply drawing out the logical implication of this emphasis on the inwardness of ethics when he insisted on the need for man to be in the right relationship with God. 'Faith by itself, if it has no works, is dead', as the Epistle of James says.[14] But works that are not the expression of a right disposition are counterfeit coin. And for St Paul a right disposition depends on openness to the grace of God which is the life of faith.

This is where we must start: by identification with man in his inward moral predicament and by spelling out the distinctive Christian understanding of what a man is meant to be. But clearly we must go much further. We have to ask how this affords a foundation for conduct which is both public and social. Here we face a paradoxical state of affairs. The insistence of many of the younger generation that they should be free to express their passions in any way they wish is often coupled with an idealism about economic and social justice, race relations and international peace which puts the majority of older and more conventional people to shame. It is not without significance that the word 'obscenity' is coming back into the vocabulary of the young, applied not to sexual aberrations but to events in Vietnam, Nigeria, Rhodesia and South Africa, to racial strife in the great cities, and above all to the growing disparity between the rich and the poor nations. Passionately rejecting conventional codes of conduct which seem to have allowed these obscenities to happen, those who storm the streets in protest marches and organize 'sit-ins' are searching for a new morality which gets to grips with the world as it really is.

Christians must understand this as one of the most hopeful signs of our times. But there is another side to the picture. Idealism may turn into a form of escapism, a substitute for facing the deep moral dilemma of contemporary society. Christians have been castigated, with no little justification, for their individualistic pietism and neglect of the great social issues. That is a verdict which has to be taken to heart with the utmost seriousness. On the other hand it is not nearly so widely recognized that the dismissal of what may be called the inwardness of ethics and rushing off to embrace some great cause are in danger of producing a moral escapism every whit as unrealistic as extreme pietism and perhaps ultimately more damaging. There is, unfortunately, plenty of evidence to suggest that much promising idealism is turning very sour indeed, infected by the delusion that it does not matter what people are in themselves so long as they support the right policies. The fact is that the poison of undisciplined self-indulgence can so drastically corrupt the most lofty aspirations. If free rein is given to uncontrolled passion, not only lust, but hatred, malice, envy, cruelty and power-hungry disregard for other people will take command. And that is what we see happening all over the world. It is no accident that frequently protests against war, racial discrimination and social injustice quickly become the policy of confrontation, the oppression of opponents and the cult of violence for its own sake. 'Nor can a bad tree bear good fruit.'[15]

What, then, is the Christian ideal of public and social conduct which stems from this understanding of man as one who needs to be inwardly transformed by the grace of God into someone who progressively cares for his fellows and their ultimate welfare? Contrasted with the philosophy of confrontation and conflict, the New Testament centres on the theme of reconciliation, properly understood not simply in terms of the vertical reconciliation of men to God, but in terms also of the horizontal reconciliation of men to one another. The theme is powerfully presented in Ephesians 2: 12–18, and extended to the whole created universe in Colossians 1: 20 and Ephesians 1: 10, where the purpose of God is declared to be 'a plan for the fullness of time, to unite all things in him, things in heaven and things on earth'.

I believe this provides us with a more comprehensive framework within which the guidelines for personal conduct and social action can be drawn than any other interpretation of the Gospel. It is fashionable nowadays to maintain with the exponents of 'situation ethics' that 'love' is the key concept in the light of which all moral questions have to be judged.[16] Clearly this is not the place to embark on a detailed discussion of a subject which merits a whole book. Suffice it to say that, in my opinion, the word has become so debased in current usage and is popularly interpreted in such sentimental and individualistic terms that it is extremely difficult to rescue it to do the job required. To tell a politician or a trade-union official that 'all you need is love' is to invite derision, and derision that is well justified in the light of the images evoked by the mention of the word. But even when it is reinterpreted in terms of active caring for other people in all sorts of situations, I question whether it sufficiently comes to grips with the range and depth of the Christian revelation. No one would deny the *prominence* of love in the New Testament. But when we come to ask what this means in the full context of the Gospel we are surely driven to recognize that it has to be interpreted within the framework of the purpose of God for man and the whole created universe, summed up in the Pauline assertion that 'God was in Christ reconciling the world to himself'.[17] This emphasis on the theme of reconciliation gives a cosmic and corporate dimension to the understanding of love as a committed concern for the welfare of others which delivers it from any individualistic, and still more from any purely sentimental, reference. It grounds love in a cosmic purpose which is not the absorption of man into an impersonal absolute, but is his growth into maturity, measured by what the writer to the Ephesians called 'the stature of the fullness of Christ'.[18] It allows for the maximum diversity in a harmonious relationship with God and everyone and everything else.

If the ideal of a reconciled universe does provide the criterion for assessing the moral problems which face everybody today, its detailed application is an immense task, and one that leaves room for a great deal of controversy. It obviously undergirds with fresh strength the protest against racial discrimination and apartheid; but it renders more than problematical the attempt to enforce the American idea of a free society on South East Asia. In the whole field of inter-personal relations a set of questions becomes relevant that is all too often left out of account. Am I entitled to keep myself to myself? Am I free to choose my own way of life with the purely negative consideration of what will do no harm to others? Am I at liberty to write off other people as uninteresting, tiresome, difficult, and so on? These are only a few of the practical issues that arise when the ideal of a reconciled universe is taken seriously.

But the most nagging of all questions remains: is this an ethic applicable only to committed Christians? If so, what is its relevance to all those whose perplexities and struggles we are summoned to share and yet who do not profess the same faith? Obviously the full relevance of the Christian ideal depends on acceptance of the Gospel and the resolve to live by it. But it also provides a criterion in the light of which judgements regarding conduct and policy can be made in a pluralist society. This will mean the frank recognition of a double standard: what can be expected of committed Christians and what can be realistically advocated for society at large.[19] That is the price of involvement: to hold fast to the ideal and at the same time to be inextricably bound up with the predicament of ordinary people in their perplexity.

In short, the magisterial stance has to be totally abandoned.

The search for practical answers to problems of conduct and policy must be pursued in sympathetic engagement with all those who are struggling to find meaning and purpose within the chaotic world in which we are living together. While Christians have a pole star to guide them—the ideal of a perfected harmony in the kingdom of God—the application of this ideal to man's involvement in ambiguous existence is so far from straightforward that any dogmatism which rests on the assumption of a privileged position or inside knowledge is wholly out of place. With everyone else, we are fumbling seekers, looking for 'the city which has foundations, whose builder and maker is God'.[20] It is from such a perspective that the Church must be incarnated in the moral quest.

This leads directly to the third and in some ways most fundamental transformation of attitude which the doctrine of the Incarnation requires of us. Earlier I implied that most people do not *feel* that the Church is really identified with them. The sense of apartness is at a far deeper level than that of the intellect; it is at the very well-springs of human life where emotion rules to a degree which we have simply not measured. What is a commonplace in psychology has hardly come to the surface in ecclesiastical circles. By and large, church leaders have been frightened of facing the emotional basis of religion, lest they should be engulfed in the extravagances which have characterized the revivalist movements. So Christianity has become intellectualized and it is therefore not surprising that the Church has generally appeared cold and aloof. As David Edwards pertinently observes, 'A realistic assessment of religion (or of atheism) must begin where people begin—not with ideas but with emotions, shaped as these have been by everyday experiences and by all the subtle influences of home and school, work and friends'.[21]

This reluctance to come to terms with the emotional depths of man's nature is compounded by the Englishman's distrust of any display of feeling. To keep a stiff upper lip, to hide behind a façade of casual play-acting, to preserve the appearance of nonchalance at all costs, these have long been associated with the image of respectability. 'Thou shalt not expose thyself to other people' has been the unwritten first commandment of the well-bred Britisher. And the Established Church has not unnaturally led the way in conforming to this standard.

But the Christian Gospel is not addressed to the surface of life, to its conventionalities and pretences. It is relevant to the whole man in the very depths of his being, and unless it breaks through to the inner springs of human nature and awakens the profoundest emotional response, it will obviously appear to be a hollow sham. One of the most significant phenomena in the contemporary religious scene is the spectacular growth of the Pentecostalist movement in almost every part of the world. Whatever its theological deficiencies and uncontrolled enthusiasm, it does seem to have rung a bell in the hearts of a host of people to whom traditional churchmanship has made no appeal. This is a fact which it is sheer folly to ignore or dismiss with superior indifference. It constitutes a challenge of the very first importance to any Christian thinking about renewal.

If we are to come to grips with this, the most crucial and at the same time elusive issue of Christian involvement, we have to take our cue from the identification of Jesus with the men and women of his time. We are told that 'the sight of the people moved him to pity; they were like sheep without a shepherd, harassed and helpless'.[22] The word rendered 'pity' is extremely difficult to translate, and the version of the New English Bible almost certainly gives the wrong impression. The original reference is to the stirring of the deepest feelings, and it is likely that the Authorised rendering of 'compassion' gets nearer to the heart of the matter; for compassion literally means 'feeling with'. Jesus was not merely sorry for people; he felt with them, imaginatively sharing their inmost emotions. He knew what it was like to be them.

At the risk of tedious repetition let me underscore that it is the estrangement of the Church from most ordinary folk, not at the level of the intellect but at the level of the emotions, which is the greatest hindrance to communicating the Gospel today. Indeed, communication that is envisaged as crossing a barrier is no communication at all. What is required is sharing, and this can take place only when the barriers are down and people know they are on common ground. In other words, it is on the basis of discovering what it is to be human and share in real human life that the Church can be the Church of the Incarnation. To come alive to the depths of the humanity of Jesus is essential to Christian renewal.

All this is easier said than done. What does it mean in practice? The answer in part lies in a radical reappraisal of our ecclesiastical structures which now largely militate against the identification of which I have been speaking. This will be our concern in the chapters that follow. But first we need to set our sights and ask what general change of attitude is required to give us the vision and the impetus to break through those structures in which we now find ourselves imprisoned.

If identification in feeling is what we are impelled to seek, then a reorientation of imagination is required. One of the principal hindrances to this is the dichotomy between the Church and the world which has become part and parcel of the outlook of most Christians. We speak of the Christian message to the world, the Church's ministry to the world and so on; and our very buildings, which we call churches, suggest a separation from ordinary men and women in their common life. This terminology, with its accompanying imagery, needs to be decisively rejected. The Church *is* the world—in depth: the depth of commitment to Christ and witness to him at the heart of the world's life. The Church is not to be found behind closed doors and up high steps on the corner of the street. It is at the kitchen sink, at the factory bench, in the offices, in the hospitals, in the schools, in the shops and travelling on public transport. There is the Church, coterminous with the world, but grounded in Christ. To think imaginatively in this way is the precondition of identification with others.

The emphasis I have placed on incarnation, identification and involvement inevitably raises the question whether the adoption of such an approach will not hopelessly compromise the Gospel. The Church, it will be said, could so conform to the world as to be absorbed by it. Did not the apostle warn his readers 'Do not be conformed to this world but be transformed by the renewal of your mind'?[23] The danger is an obvious one, but it is avoided no less at the cost of the Gospel by the policy of separation and withdrawal. There is an inescapable tension in the commission of Jesus when he tells his disciples that they are to be in the world but not of it. A way has to be found between Scylla and Charybdis; for on either rock the Church will come to wreckage. How are we to hold to the truth that is embodied in Christ without making pretentious claims for the truth of our limited comprehension of the divine revelation? How are we to bear witness to the ideal of Christian perfection and the kingdom of God while acknowledging our participation in the sin of mankind? How are we to live as members of the redeemed community and at the same time enter sympathetically into the feelings and aspirations of those who as yet have not woken up to any dimension of reality save the surface of the world's passing show? As we have seen, the clue to answering these questions is to be found in the ministry of our Lord himself. The embodiment in the Church of the insight this affords is never anything but precarious; for its members share all the human frailties. Nevertheless we dare to believe that this is the form of Christ's continuing incarnation.

Chapter Two

Obsolete Structures

While Christian renewal primarily involves a change of approach to basic issues, it has to be embodied in organizational structures at the international, national, regional and local levels which will really serve the purpose of the Church. This brings us face to face with the almost unbelievable web of entanglement in which Christians find themselves enmeshed. The machinery of government and industry is under constant criticism for its bureaucracy, entrenched conservatism and wastage of resources, but all this pales into insignificance when compared with the sheer inflexibility and inefficiency of our anachronistic ecclesiastical structures.

Quite apart from questions that need to be raised about overlapping bureaucracy and the wastage of resources, the thing that sticks out like a sore thumb on the British scene, to go no further afield, is the obsolescence of existing denominational divisions inherited from a past age and no longer reflecting the realities of the present situation. The convictions that unite and divide Christians cross the ecclesiastical frontiers, and our administrative machinery more often than not obscures the facts with which we have to reckon, besides impeding the Church's true mission.

The truth is that many Christians in all the ecclesiastical bodies find themselves much closer to others of an outwardly different persuasion than they do to a large number of their fellow communicants. Agreements cross the denominational frontiers and disagreements divide Christians within the denominational framework on strikingly similar grounds. In other words, the lines of demarcation are horizontal rather than vertical, and this makes nonsense of the structures in which we are at present imprisoned.

This may be seen by directing attention to six major issues which cut across the ecclesiastical frontiers and far outweigh in importance most, if not all, of those tenets which have traditionally separated Christians from one another, and to a large extent continue to do so. Moreover the interpretation of distinctive denominational emphases is in general profoundly affected by the attitude taken to these more basic questions.

1. On any showing, the approach to truth is surely fundamental. There are those in every communion who hold that verbal propositions, whether in the Scriptures, the Creeds or Ecclesiastical Formulae, are absolutely and unconditionally true. They are not subject to revision because they are completely adequate to that which they are designed to express. On the other hand there are those who insist that all concepts and formulations of them are relative in the sense that they are inadequate to the richness of that to which they bear witness. This, as we have seen, does not make them untrue; they are more or less true: an inevitable corollary of admitting the limitations of thought and language. Those who adopt the first position will be divided from one another as they disagree on what propositions are to be taken as exhaustive and final; in other words, there is a built-in divisiveness in this attitude due to the limitations of human insight. But the basic divide does not lie there. It is between those whose view of truth is fundamentally different: between those with a closed and open approach.

At this crucial point denominational and confessional party labels prove totally irrelevant. Catholics and Evangelicals are to be found on both sides of the line.

2. Christians are also united and divided across and within the ecclesiastical frontiers in their approach to the relationship between grace and faith. Manifestly this is one of the great unsolved problems of theology. All down the centuries thinkers have wrestled with the question how man's salvation is the work of God without making nonsense of human responsibility. There is no slick answer, as the Pelagian and Arminian controversies make abundantly plain, not to speak of the mountain of books and articles which have been published on the subject. In the end grace and faith have to be held together in delicate balance, and this is by no means easy to preserve. Inevitably there are bound to be differences of emphasis, and Christians find themselves divided according to whether they think of faith within the context of grace or vice versa. There is all the difference in the world between insisting that the grace of God in redemption is available only to those who by a deliberate act of repentance and faith turn to him, and on the other hand holding that the grace of God in redemption is the birthright of all men which needs to be appropriated by repentance and faith, but which is their God-given possession through the finished work of Christ.

Those who lay emphasis on the first of these approaches will tend to stress the supreme importance of personal evangelism; for everything else, if not regarded as a waste of time, shades into virtual insignificance when compared with the supreme importance of saving souls from destruction. On the other hand, those who see the divine purpose in creation and redemption as concerned with the reconciliation of the whole created universe and its consummation in Christ, while not minimizing the importance of personal commitment, will set this within a context of God's gracious activity enfolding the frailty of all human response. The contrast is not really between an evangelical concern for evangelism and a radical concern for the redemption of the social order. That is far too superficial a polarization. The basic tension is between faith conceived as the condition of grace, or at least as the inseparable corollary of grace, and faith as response to the all-encompassing grace of God.

Incidentally, baptismal theology is inevitably affected by the attitude taken to this fundamental question, and it is by no means clear that the real difference is any longer between those who have inherited the paedo-baptist tradition and those who have stood for the baptism of believers only. The underlying issue is again the relation of grace to faith, and as the subject of baptism is investigated in the light of the empirical facts, denominational distinctions tend to become increasingly blurred. Paedo-baptists have the problem of the host of infants who grow up to adolescence and adulthood without any allegiance to the Faith, while Baptists are faced with the responsibility of giving some account of the church context in which faith is nurtured and awakened, as well as with recognizing their own problem of the large number of those who fall away after making a public profession. We are unlikely to make much further progress in understanding the rite of Christian initiation and its relation to the doctrine of the Church until we have grasped more clearly the fundamental theological issue underlying the debate. When this happens, it is by no means obvious that those who find themselves in basic agreement will be in the same denominational camp.

3. Thirdly, there is the question of the Christian's attitude to the secular order. Some years ago the late Philippe Maury, when Secretary of the World Student Christian Federation, said in private conversation that he believed the basic issue uniting and dividing Christians was their attitude to the world. On the one hand there are those who have given up the world for lost and regard the Church as a kind of fortress in an alien land, the beleaguered garrison stretching out hands to rescue individuals and bring them within the security of the citadel. On the other hand there are those who believe that the whole world belongs to God in virtue of creation and redemption, and that the Church is to be conceived as the scattered community, claiming to find the kingdom in the most unexpected places.

This difference of outlook is obviously reflected in the current debate on the nature of Christian mission. If the Church is regarded as the ark of God, stretching out hands to those drowning in the troubled seas of the world, mission will be seen as essentially a rescue operation. God will be thought of as confined within the Church, active only through its agencies, and having forsaken the world of his creation. Mission is then the Church's mission, and only the mission of God in so far as the Church is directly involved. On the contrary, a growing number of Christians insist that we have to take our stand with what God is doing in the world. Mission is his engagement in the whole created order and it is the calling of the Church to discern where and how he is at work and to become identified with him in what he is doing.

This has come to be articulated in recent discussion initiated by the World Council of Churches as the *missio Dei*—God's mission to the world. Instead of the familiar order

God-Church-world, we are bidden to see that it should be reversed as God-world-Church. The thesis is most clearly set forth in a lecture by a prominent Lutheran theologian in which he asks whether mission is the work of God or the task of the Church.[1] Although he is not uncritical of the answer, he puts it succinctly as follows:

> Mission is understood correctly only when its theological locus is recognized as being the doctrine of God rather than ecclesiology. Mission is not a function of the Church; the Church is, instead, a function of God's mission. God as a missionary God is not simply the initiator of the mission of the Church; on the contrary, he wishes to invoke the Church's mission in the mission. The Church must orient itself in its sending to God's ambassador, to Jesus Christ, the missionary.[2]

Once this thesis is grasped, it is obvious that a wide gulf is opened up between those who accept it and those who begin the other way round. Two radically different views of the relationship between the Church and the world in the providence of God are at stake.

Admittedly I have drawn the lines with the maximum of sharpness, and for most people the issue has not yet been defined with such stark clarity. The distinction between the two approaches is often blurred and it is by no means easy to identify where many Christians stand in relation to the question. Moreover there is no clear-cut alignment of those who hold strong convictions on one side or the other with their views on different matters. We should not expect to find theological parcels neatly tied up with string. In particular, some conservative evangelicals have in recent years become increasingly concerned with questions of international peace and social justice, refusing to be identified with the pietism that has characterized so many who share their convictions in other respects; though this emphasis is probably to be interpreted as an extension of personal evangelism rather than a radical rethinking of mission. However that may be, it is broadly true that world-denying Christians tend to be found amongst those who take an absolutist attitude to religious truth and emphasize grace within the context of faith. On the other hand, a world-affirming outlook is in general allied to openness to truth and the conviction that faith has always to be understood as response to the all-encompassing grace of God. Here again polarization crosses the denominational boundaries, rendering the latter more and more problematical.

4. Fourth, there is the sacramental principle. I choose to speak of this rather than of the Sacraments because basic theological attitudes underlie differences on specific points of doctrine. There are those who conceive Christianity in inward and spiritual terms, the visible and tangible being somewhat arbitrary expressions of that which is really important. Consequently questions of external order are thought to be matters of convention rather than embodiments of fundamental principle. By contrast, there are those within all the Christian Confessions who hold that the spiritual cannot be divorced from the material because this makes nonsense of the structure of existence and in any case is ruled out of court by the doctrine of the Incarnation. In Christ Jesus the Word of God became enfleshed, earthed in the life of One who was fully man and revealed the Father within the limitations of concrete physical existence. And the Church is his body, incarnated in the visible form of ecclesiastical structures, however deformed these have

become through human blindness and intransigence. But there is no escape from incarnation into a purely spiritual realm. The distinction that is often drawn between the visible and the invisible Church has a limited usefulness in pointing to the underlying unity of faith and life which transcends the barriers of denominational allegiance, but it is dangerously misleading if it allows us to avoid asking serious theological questions and to acquiesce in structural patterns which hide rather than reveal the Christ who wills to be embodied in every age and place.

In the last resort, the really significant differences between Christians in regard to church order do not lie between those who accept episcopal or non-episcopal ministries, between those who adopt Independency, Presbyterianism or Hierarchy in church government, or between those who interpret the Eucharist sacrificially and those who regard it as a service of memorial. The basic issue is the sacramental principle, the relation between the inward and the outward; and it is largely a waste of time trying to communicate across the ecclesiastical frontiers when there is no clarity or agreement within the denominational framework about underlying presuppositions.

5. It is clear that another subject on which the alignment is increasingly horizontal rather than vertical is that of liturgy. On the one hand, there are those who appear content to abide by and defend the forms of worship which they have inherited from the past, and on the other those who insist that liturgical reform is an urgent priority if worship is to be an authentic expression of corporate Christian devotion. Clearly this difference of outlook is found within all the Christian communions. Many, from Roman

Catholics to Quakers, are resistant to any suggestion of change, seeing in it either an invitation to licence or the betrayal of spontaneity as the case may be. Conversely liturgical reformers, while insisting on the importance of tradition, structure and discipline, are anxious to allow the maximum scope for experiment and for making worship a genuine expression of contemporary aspirations. The results are surprising and sometimes shocking to those who find it difficult to conceive how any departure from the accepted norm could possibly be justified. What are they to make of Baptist congregations adopting the traditional structure of the mass as the normal form of Sunday morning service culminating in the act of communion, or of the abandonment of the seven traditional monastic offices at the Augustinian house in Eindhoven, Holland, and their replacement by morning and evening services drawn up by the monks themselves?[3] The old landmarks seem to be disappearing.

6. All five points obviously affect the approach to Christian unity. For those who take the first of the alternative positions outlined above, unity is generally envisaged only amongst those who share an unambiguous statement of belief, who have had an identifiable kind of inward experience, or who have adopted a particular attitude to the world and the Church. This is to be distinguished from the standpoint of those who see the real Church emerging from the structures of the past and finding a new unity in outward expression which transcends anything we now know in our separated and imprisoned state. The work of the Holy Spirit is seen as bringing something new to birth which will gather up all our partial insights, as far as they are valid, and, which while still the pilgrim Church, will be a

more comprehensive community than anything that has been realized in the past.

In the light of this consensus on fundamental issues which crosses all the existing ecclesiastical frontiers, the attempt to justify inherited denominational divisions suggests the stricture of Jesus about 'straining out a gnat and swallowing a camel'.[4] But while this may be admitted, perhaps reluctantly, strong resistance is certainly going to be encountered to any suggestion that these theological considerations justify, still less impel, a radical restructuring of the Church as we know it today. Quite apart from the vested interests involved, which are a formidable obstacle to any serious consideration of such a possibility, we have to reckon with a number of arguments advanced in favour of nothing being done to alter the *status quo*.

1. In the first place, it will be said that most people are so inherently conservative and so emotionally attached to what is familiar that they will resist any radical changes in allegiance, sticking tenaciously to the old lines of demarcation, whatever the theological arguments may be to the contrary. If any attempt were made to force the issue and urge an ecclesiastical realignment, the denominational hackles would rise and all the hard-worn doctrinal tenets would be trotted out to bolster up things as they are. These articles of faith might well be a smoke-screen concealing the desire to preserve certain sociological patterns rather than face the unpalatable facts, for doctrine can notoriously be used to escape from uncomfortable theological reflection. We are all past masters at producing plausible excuses for indefensible positions.

The outcome of the controversy that would result from taking the lid off, we shall be told, would be even further division within an already divided Church. While some might be prepared for realignment on a realistic basis, the experience of reunion schemes shows that there would be a continuing rump of all the existing denominations, not to speak of the encouragement given to the further proliferation of sects. The last state of the man would be worse than the first.

While there is some substance in this argument, much can be said on the other side. Every effort should certainly be made to ensure that the new reformation through which we are passing does not lead to further disastrous divisions, but we may still have to reckon with Milton's famous words that 'there must be many schisms and many dissections in the quarry and in the timber ere the house of God can be built.'[5] If we must live with division in the foreseeable future, is there not a strong case for insisting that it be along realistic lines and not on the inherited basis of an age now past?

But there is more to be said than that. Events are forcing the issue, and they cannot be resisted. More and more people are finding their church allegiance in congregations of mixed denominational background. In a society where moving house is a frequent occurrence a growing proportion of those who do so either forsake the Church altogether or tend to associate with a congregation of like-minded people. Anglicans, Presbyterians, Methodists, Baptists and Congregationalists with a mixture of Salvationists and others often make up the membership of a church on a new housing estate or in a retirement neighbourhood. The realignment is already taking place, though in almost accidental fashion and undirected by any profound convictions. In the meanwhile those who could lead a significant and purposeful reorientation often remain imprisoned within the old structures for fear of rocking the boat.

2. A second argument that will undoubtedly be advanced is that, whatever their defects, the existing denominations do manage to hold together people of widely diverse views. If structural reorganization is pressed and reunion schemes go much further, we are told that this will lead to a fatal rift between Catholics and conservative Evangelicals, not to mention the possible impact on those opting for the middle road, who refuse to be identified with either wing, but who through loyalty to specific denominational emphases might feel compelled to be continuing Methodists, Baptists and so on. As it is, they constitute the bridge between Catholics and conservative Evangelicals within the existing structures.

There is, of course, no small measure of truth in this contention; and the Church of England is often cited as a particularly striking example of comprehensive breadth. But if we are concerned to have a framework within which the maximum possible diversity is ensured, there does not seem to be any compelling reason why this should be wastefully and unrealistically multiplied. Surely we need to grasp the nettle and ask whether the fact that different denominations have been able to hold together widely divergent views within one organizational structure does not mean that we have reached the position when we can see that one structure could embrace them all. Of course, there are many difficulties to be overcome, and, human nature being what it is, there will be many dissidents. Nevertheless, it is high time that Free Churchmen, who profess to cherish diversity, should be prepared to face their sociological prejudices—and these as much as liturgical or theological questions affect their relationship to Anglicans—and find their home in a reformed Church of England. This, of course, entails an equal degree of flexibility on the part of Anglicans: a flexibility that is all too obviously inhibited by the inherited rigidity of their ecclesiastical tradition.

3. A third objection arises directly out of what has just been said. Not a few will vigorously react against any suggestion of a monolithic organization. This, it is held, is exactly what we do not want and we should resist with all the force at our command any proposal that appears to be directed to that end. So far from the multiplicity of structures being something to be deplored, they have a positive advantage in ensuring a variety of church life and serve as an insurance against ecclesiastical totalitarianism.

While such an argument on first impact is bound to be appealing, it is, I believe, open to devastating criticism. It is by no means plain that variety is best conserved by multiplying bureaucratic organizations. On the contrary, I have suggested that the purpose of any acceptable ecclesiastical structure should be to allow for the widest possible range of churchmanship within a common framework. This contention is further strengthened if we agree with the forecast of Harvey Cox in *The Secular City* that in the future 'church unity ... will not be a matter of the divisions between denominations, but of the relationship between highly differentiated expressions of the same Church.'[6]

Further, does not the argument against the monolithic organization betray an exaggerated view, all too deeply rooted, of the importance of ecclesiastical centralization over against the life of the Church at the grass roots? To hear some people talking one might suppose that Christian influence is primarily exerted by committees meeting in London and that it is the function of those at the local and parish level to supply the means whereby the machine is kept working and made ever more complex. The fact is that ecclesiastical organization at the national and regional levels is necessary only in so far as it enables Christians the better to bear witness to their faith where they live and work, with the additional responsibility of bringing their combined influence to bear on major matters of policy. What we need here is a sense of proportion. I am not for a moment suggesting that we can dispense with large scale organization nor that to engage in it is to dirty one's hands with something sub-Christian. I am simply urging that we should see it cut down to size in relation to the witness of the Church in the world. It is a means to an end, not an end in itself; and, as such, it should be as simple and efficient as we can make it. As things stand, the Church is getting more and more top-heavy, with more and more energy being poured into co-ordination and less and less to co-ordinate. Our sense of priorities needs reversing.

However we may assess these three objections and the arguments advanced against them, we have to face the fact that the ramifications of ecclesiastical organization are now so wasteful in terms of men and money that they are in grave danger of breaking down altogether. The signs are on the wall for anyone to read. With a diminishing membership and rising costs some church organizations have reached or almost reached the peak of their effort to maintain the existing structures; and they continue to do so for the time being only at the cost of woefully underpaying the clergy and ministers whom they so prodigally deploy.

Consider the facts. Confining ourselves to manageable

proportions, let us take a look at the major non-Roman Catholic Churches of England and Wales. In doing so we leave out of the account the Orthodox and Lutherans, who constitute comparatively small groups of Christians with predominantly European affiliations, and the large number of those associated with sects of one kind and another, for whom reliable statistics are difficult to obtain. But the latter omission merely underlines the bewildering complexity of ecclesiastical machinery.

Restricting ourselves, then, to the Anglican and Free Churches, each of these has its own headquarters, all with a wide range of departments responsible for promoting work amongst men, women, young people and children, or dealing with finance, property, training and recognition of candidates for the ministry, literature, moral and social questions, international affairs and a hundred and one other things. Some of these concerns are co-ordinated in the British Council of Churches and the residual responsibilities retained by the Free Church Federal Council. Alongside these are the missionary societies, each again with its own headquarters, departments and staff, and all the various Church-sponsored agencies of an interdenominational character, like the British and Foreign Bible Society, the YMCA, the YWCA, the National Council for Christian Education, the Student Christian Movement, the Inter-Varsity Fellowship and a host of others too numerous to mention. Almost all, if not all, these headquarters have their ramifications in various degrees of complexity throughout the regions of the British Isles, and trying to see the picture as a whole is rather like attempting to map a jungle.

Of course, I do not wish to minimize the importance of adequate and efficient organization to sustain the mission of the Church. That should go without saying. But it is a very different matter to acquiesce in the structures that have 'growed up like Topsy' and not to face the full impact of their bewildering proliferation. Perhaps the best method of bringing home the wastage of limited resources is to consider the way in which the overseas enterprise of the Churches is conducted. This is not meant to suggest that the missionary societies are the most glaring examples of prodigality. On the contrary, a good case could be made out for maintaining that they compare more than favourably with other ecclesiastical bodies in deploying the resources available to them within the structures in which they operate. My reason for focusing attention on them is that their published statistics provide the clearest picture of the cost of a multiplicity of organizations in relation to the actual work being done at the grass roots. From a conspectus of the information available, it may be possible to draw some significant conclusions.

The following table is restricted to those members of the Conference of British Missionary Societies from whom the relevant statistics are most easily available. This does not give the complete picture because, apart from the very considerable Roman Catholic involvement, there are a number of other organizations related to the CBMS as well as conservative Evangelical missions which are unwilling to be associated with it. However, as we shall argue later, those who opt for an extreme conservative position are on the whole unlikely to be willing to face any sort of rationalization of structures, insisting that the preservation of their identity as safeguarding a particular doctrine has an importance overriding all other considerations. Nevertheless, the existence of these separate organizations simply

Name of Society	*Year*	*Expenditure (to nearest £)* Total	Home organization	*Approx. number of serving missionaries†*
Baptist Missionary Society	1966–7	£417,174	£ 81,164	283
Church Missionary Society	1967	936,152	210,360	648
Church of Scotland	1967	692,662	96,920	353
Church's Ministry among the Jews	1967	82,559	22,000	94
Congregational Council for World Mission	1967–8	473,793	61,326	236
Episcopal Church in Scotland	1967	30,054	5,034	17
Friends Service Council	1967	187,824	43,366	85
Jerusalem & The East Mission	1966	46,366	16,484	30
Methodist Missionary Society	1967	1,370,610	148,289	440
Oxford Mission to Calcutta	1967	27,058	4,570	37
Presbyterian Church of England	1966	67,348	11,631	41
Presbyterian Church of Wales	1967	48,142	6,074	15
South American Missionary Society	1967	93,222	23,672	108
Sudan Interior Mission	1966–7	89,590*	15,357*	600
United Society for the Propagation of the Gospel	1967	1,035,242	220,469	856 (1968)
	TOTAL	5,597,796	966,716	3843

* SIM total = $\frac{2}{3}$ of the single figure given for 18 months.

† The total of serving missionaries is very approximate in that some societies do not indicate whether wives are or are not included. (The Methodist Missionary Society figure definitely excludes them.)

means that the jungle is thicker and more overgrown than the appended analysis suggests.

Although the societies break down their statistics in different ways, making it hard to achieve consistency in this table, the foregoing figures speak for themselves. In one year 15 societies spent £5,597,796 to support 3843 missionaries overseas. In terms of home organization this cost £966,716 leaving out of account the capital value of all the headquarters involved. The second figure is the crucial one to examine. How much could be saved if some, if not all, of these operations could be rationalized? When one considers the number of parallel departments concerned with education, finance, recruitment, promotion amongst children, youth, men and women, not to speak of the portfolios responsible for overlapping areas of the world, one is bound to ask whether this is not a luxury which is inexcusable in the light of the resources available and the need for strategic planning of the global mission of the Church. Placed within the context of the poverty of the third world, the question becomes that much more urgent. In the sight of God have we any right to be acquiescent?

But that is not all. In this country alone there are ten Anglican missionary societies, and this takes no account of Anglican involvement in those interdenominational agencies which are not affiliated with the Conference of British Missionary Societies. What are the compelling reasons for their separate existence? Undoubtedly excuses can be found in terms of doctrinal emphasis, historical origins and concern for special areas. But do these add up to a real justification for continued separation with all that that entails?

This leads to a more basic question which in different degrees affects every one of the societies named in the table.

Historically they arose out of a concern to awaken the Church in these islands to their responsibility for the unevangelized areas overseas. But much water has flowed beneath the bridge in the intervening years. The world Church has become a reality, not least because of the imaginative pioneering of the missionary societies, and in our own day we have come to see that it is in a missionary situation everywhere. 'Mission to six continents' is increasingly becoming the watchword. But the societies which have largely been instrumental in bringing this about have as yet paid little more than lip service to what they profess. The logic of the development of the past sixty years since the Edinburgh Conference of 1910, which gave the initial impetus to the modern ecumenical movement, is that mission is the calling of the whole Church in its interdependence across the world; and structurally that means the identification of the missionary societies with the Churches of which they are part.

A first step was taken in this direction when the International Missionary Council was integrated with the World Council of Churches, which now has its department of mission and evangelism. But progress has been slow in implementing the policy at the national level. The Presbyterian Church of England has its Overseas Missions Committee, and the way forward for others has been shown by the structural integration of the former London Missionary Society with the newly constituted Congregational Church in the Congregational Council of World Mission. But the full consequences of these developments have yet to be taken to heart. A wide gulf remains between the thinking of missionary leaders and the understanding of ministers and men and women in the pew. Christians at large need to see that the mission of the Church in the urban and rural areas of Britain and Africa, Asia and Latin America is indivisible.[7] Only then will the process of structural rationalization be accelerated and the resources of the Church be marshalled for global mission. In the meanwhile attention must be clearly focused on the anachronism of the separation between Church and missionary society wherever that continues to obtain.

I want to emphasize that I have concentrated on the missionary societies not because I believe that they represent the worst features of organizational wastage, but because their published statistics afford the clearest illustration of the tangled web of the ecclesiastical network. It is much more difficult to get at the facts with respect to the stewardship of denominational resources in this country. Not all the Churches attempt to publish comprehensive figures, but some indication of the enormous deployment of manpower and money can be gathered from the statistics of the largest and smallest of the major bodies. In *The Church of England Year Book* for 1967 it is recorded that in the year ended 31 December 1964 £31,576,000 was raised and expended for all purposes in the provinces of Canterbury and York. This included £1,363,000 contributed for overseas missions but, deducting that amount, we find that £30,213,000 was spent on maintaining the diocesan and parish system served by 15,444 full-time and 2443 part-time dignitaries and clergymen.[8] The Reports of Committees and other papers submitted to the General Assembly of the Presbyterian Church of England in 1968 show an expenditure of £1,022,602 covering 15 presbyteries (including the presbytery of Malaysia) employing 282 ministers to 311 congregations, comprising 65,066 communicant members. Taking these figures as a guide to the total commitment of the non-Roman Churches in England, one may reasonably ask whether effectiveness in mission is at all commensurate with the expenditure and deployment of the resources available.

The answer becomes starkly apparent when we turn to the local scene. What are we to say about the multiplicity of church buildings, for the most part standing unused for the greater part of the week and then in the majority of cases only fractionally occupied when services are held? Bearing in mind the rising costs of maintenance, how are we to defend this vast investment in bricks and mortar?[9] What justification is there for the large army, albeit a declining army, of clergy and ministers conducting worship for sparse congregations at the same time, with all the hours of preparation involved? Can we complacently accept the dissipation of energy resulting from unco-ordinated ministries at a time when isolation and loneliness are so often the parson's lot? The force of these questions can be brought home by considering specific cases. A commission recently charged with examining the mission of the Church in the inner city confines of Birmingham discovered that within a two-mile radius of the district of Handsworth, populated by large numbers of immigrants and people living in apartment blocks or sub-standard housing, over forty separate Churches were at work, each with its own set of premises! The pitiful inadequacy of what they are all doing is patent to see. But what hope is there for any effective mission without concerted action, which is rendered impossible as long as rigid denominational barriers and conservative attachment to old buildings and antiquated structures are maintained?

The example I have cited could be repeated over and

over again up and down the country. In cities, towns and villages throughout the land this prodigal wastage of Christian resources is a scandal of the first magnitude. Nor is it simply due to the unco-ordinated overlapping of Churches of different traditions. The denominational structures themselves are far too inflexible to measure up to the needs of the situation. This is particularly obvious in the case of the Anglican communion. Based upon the parochial system with its rigidly drawn geographical boundaries, the Church of England as at present constituted is unable to deploy its resources in relation to changing social patterns and real human need. The full extent of the problem was brought to light by Leslie Paul in the now famous report associated with his name.[10] He found that the urban dioceses were woefully understaffed compared with those comprising mainly rural districts, and the figures he gave are a startling commentary on the obsolescence of a system organized to cover ground rather than people. According to him, 10.5 per cent of the population are grouped in livings of under 2000 inhabitants, and are served by 38.2 per cent of the parochial clergy; 55.8 per cent of the population are grouped in livings of between 2000 and 9999 inhabitants and are served by 45.2 per cent of the parochial clergy; while 33.7 per cent of the population are grouped in livings of 10,000 inhabitants and over and enjoy the services of only 16.6 per cent of the clergy.[11]

These figures speak for themselves. They show how geography, rather than the need of human beings, so often dictates the strategy of the Church. This is not due to a failure of those in office to see what the problem is or a lack of desire to remedy it; the issue is much more complicated than that. As the Paul Report makes abundantly clear, the fault lies in the structures devised to meet an entirely different situation: the settled rural communities of the pre-industrial period. In particular, the author focuses attention on three major factors which, as long as they obtain, make it almost impossible to take any radical action.

The first of these is the parson's freehold, which guarantees the encumbent's tenure of his living at his own discretion, inhibits the redrawing of parochial boundaries, and renders the introduction of team ministries extremely difficult. The second is the system of patronage, whereby individuals and corporate bodies have the gift of benefices outside ecclesiastical jurisdiction and without any necessary regard to the concern of the Church as a whole.[12] The third factor is the establishment itself: the legal subservience of Church to State, which renders any proposed reforms subject to most complicated procedures, liable to frustrate the best intentions of those who initiate them.[13] In other words the structure of the Church of England makes it exceedingly hard to introduce a more rationally planned use of manpower, money and buildings.

The Free Churches have their own problems. Methodists are probably in the best position to cope with a rapidly changing situation because of their centralization of authority in Conference, which at least makes a planned use of manpower possible. At the same time they have had their own share of frustration since the union of United Methodists, Wesleyan Methodists and Primitive Methodists in 1933. It is one thing to marry denominational structures; it is another to ensure that congregations really come together at the local level; and redundant Methodist Churches are to be found all over the country, tenaciously clinging to their separate existence.

Baptists and Congregationalists are saddled with a long tradition of independency, each company of believers claiming the privilege of determining its own policy and often doing so without much regard to their fellow Baptists and Congregationalists, let alone Christians of other persuasions. In recent years there has been a marked shift towards recognizing the fact of interdependence, and the coming into being of the Congregational Church of England and Wales and the negotiations opened between this body and the Presbyterian Church of England are welcome signs of a more realistic approach. But those most closely associated with these developments would be the first to admit that they are only at the beginning of a limited integration. There is no guarantee that attitudes will change in many places at the grass roots. As for Baptists, independency remains a major obstacle to planned co-operation, in spite of the growth in influence of the central organization at both national and regional levels, mainly through its area superintendents.

When all these factors are taken together and the scene viewed as a whole, we have to admit that so far little more has been done than tinkering with a shambles. In a rapidly changing society the Church is being extremely slow to do anything to rationalize its obsolescent structures, and it stands condemned for the prodigal wastage of its resources in the face of human need. Let us face it. This is sin, and sin writ large. It is the nemesis that follows from the divided denominational structures which we have inherited from the past. And the time has come to count the cost.

Finally the case I have been arguing can be powerfully reinforced from a somewhat different angle. When we take a broad view of the missionary outreach of the non-Roman

Churches in the British Isles, we are bound to confess that large sections of the population are virtually untouched by organized Christianity. This has been so for generations as far as the main industrial areas are concerned and the same is increasingly becoming true of the countryside. The strength of the Churches is principally in suburban districts and to a much lesser extent on the new housing estates. The point has frequently been made that the working class has not become estranged from organized Christianity; it has never had a real hold on this major sector of the population for more than 100 years.[14]

The implications of this have been clearly spelt out by the American, Gibson Winter, in his book *The Suburban Captivity of the Churches*.[15] He is, of course, concerned with the situation in his own country, but what he has to say has, *mutatis mutandis*, direct relevance to the British scene. As far as the big cities are concerned, the parallel is close, and Gibson Winter is undoubtedly right in claiming that this is where the crucial battle for the soul of the nation is to be engaged. It is not merely that these are the centres of large population where unchurched multitudes live; they are also the locus of social ferment and changing patterns of society which will determine the shape of things to come. If the Church continues to abdicate from her mission here, not only will growing sectors of the population remain untouched by Christianity, but the very structures of society will be beyond effective Christian influence. Gibson Winter's case is that suburbia is increasingly irrelevant as the major involvement of the Church. Those who live there are not self-sufficient; they depend on the city for their existence. That is where most of them earn their daily bread, and to divorce suburbia from its heart is to introduce an absolutely fatal dichotomy into the lives of those who dwell in their comfortable homes surrounded by their gardens and a cosy coterie of neighbours.[16]

No one who has any knowledge at all of the state of the inner city churches in Britain is likely to dispute the relevance of what Gibson Winter has to say to the problems we face. With few exceptions these churches are the repetition of suburbia in an alien setting. Manned by handfuls of dedicated commuters, they perpetuate forms of worship, organizations and activities in which they could equally well engage where they dwell, while the people actually living in the inner city pass them by, seeing no relevance in what they are doing to their own problems and interests. If the city-dwellers give any thought at all to the churches in their midst, they tend to regard them as little more than places where babies can be given a naming ceremony and couples have a colourful wedding. The buildings themselves often look like relics of a past age, showing the signs of dilapidation and decay, sharply contrasting with the changing face of the city as whole areas are replanned, and blocks of new offices, shops and apartments witness to the advent of technopolis.

There is no hope whatever of facing this immense challenge within our present structures of isolation. Only the most concerted and imaginative approach is likely to make the slightest impact on the great urban areas throughout the land. The irony of the situation is that the Church has the money and the manpower to do it, but our obsolete structures inhibit us at every turn. As long as we persist in thinking in parish and congregational terms, with small isolated units endeavouring to preserve their own separate identity and long-established customs, we may talk about mission till the cows come home, but we will in practice do nothing about it. The point is forcefully made by Gibson Winter when he says of the American Churches:

> Congregations are disengaged from answerable relations within the metropolis; they are autonomous bodies which claim to be answerable to God, yet seem to be answerable only to their own survival as organizations. The Churches can legitimately address human society about answerability to God and man when they are ready to face as well the question of their own responsibility.[17]

A growing number of Christian leaders, clergy, ministers and lay people have begun to realize the urgency of the situation and the need for radical change. By and large, however, the belief persists that renewal can come about without any profound alteration of the structures to which we have become accustomed. This is simply not so, and the sooner we recognize the facts the better. Indeed, that is a mild way of putting it. A changing society is rapidly outpacing the Church, which institutionally is in danger of becoming a glaring anachronism. We have not a century, nor even a decade or two, to come to terms with obsolescence. Now is the time.

Chapter Three

Breaking Through the Structures

The previous chapter presented a dismal picture. It was, of course, wide open to the criticism that it was one-sided, emphasizing the obsolescence and inadequacy of inherited ecclesiastical structures without giving due recognition to all that is being achieved through them. Furthermore, it may justifiably be said that it was full of generalizations and did not allow for some of the qualifications that could properly be made. This I frankly and freely admit. But my purpose was not to write an academic treatise, taking account of every conceivable consideration and balancing every statement with minute attention to detail. To have attempted that would have meant writing a much longer book and to have run the risk of losing sight of the wood for the trees. My concern has been to highlight the broad position in which those who are committed to the mission of the Church find themselves at the present time. Whatever the qualifications, the fact remains that our structures are singularly ill-adapted to meet the needs of the hour.

But now I must try to be positive and to suggest ways of breaking through the imprisoning framework which bedevils the whole ecclesiastical enterprise. To indulge in diagnosis is notoriously easier than to propose a cure; and all that I intend to say is necessarily tentative and exploratory. Only a fool or a fanatic would claim to have all the answers. My best hope is to direct attention to encouraging signs and growing points which may initiate discussion and lead to some further constructive action.

Where are we to begin? Should it be at the local, regional, national or international levels? My firm conviction is that we have to start at the grass roots where the mission of the Church is earthed. Unless we do that, nothing very much is likely to happen. This does not, of course, minimize the importance of structural change at all levels; it is obvious that ecclesiastical policies, whether denominational or ecumenical, determined regionally, nationally or internationally, profoundly affect the ways in which the Church at the grass roots gives expression to its mission; they are the inescapable context within which responsible decisions have to be made. Otherwise the floodgates are open to wild sectarianism. But when that has been granted, and the crucial importance of major structural changes recognized, such as the implementation of proposals for the union of Churches, the fact remains that the success or failure of these schemes depends on the way in which Churches are prepared to co-operate locally in ministry and mission.

When an army commander in time of war decides to launch an attack, he has not only to choose the best place for a breakthrough, but he has also to be prepared to exploit the new situation in which his forces, if successful, will have more room for manoeuvre. Beyond that he has to plan for advance as far as his resources allow. Initially, however, he knows that he cannot expect to penetrate the enemy lines all along the front. Many of his troops will have to be engaged in a holding operation, in which the activity of patrols and the making of limited sorties play an important part. But the breakthrough on a narrow front is crucial to the success of the campaign.

The military metaphor may not be an altogether appropriate one in every respect, but it will serve our purpose as long as it is not pressed too far. The renewal of the Church will not come through grandiose plans for reform right across the board, nor by a strategy of steady parallel advance on all fronts. It is quite unrealistic to suppose that a blueprint for renewal covering any denomination and every part of the country has the slightest chance of general acceptance or could have much relevance even if it were accepted. The problem facing all ecclesiastical assemblies is that the resolutions they adopt and the programmes they initiate have to take so many different viewpoints into account and have such wide applications that their cutting edge is almost inevitably blunted from the start. The carefully balanced statement, calculated to carry with it the maximum of support, is likely to be too cautious to provide a charter for the radical action that is required if the Church is to break out of its present imprisonment within inherited structures. The best hope is that here, there and yon creative centres of Christian renewal will emerge, where groups of people see what they are called to do, one spark lighting another till a bush fire begins to spread. In other words, I am urging the importance of local experiments in advance of the thinking of the Church as a whole, and I am pressing for the concentration of resources on such experiments at the expense, if need be, of attempting to cast the net as widely as possible. The incisive thrust should have the first priority; for events are moving too rapidly for us simply to keep pace with the slowest, let alone those who are just marking time. Elsewhere the Church will have to maintain something of a holding operation until people see what can and should be done, and are ready to break new ground.

The importance of what I have called the holding operation should not be underrated. Impatient radicals are all too prone to write off the Church as it is, dubbing it a moribund institution fit for nothing but the scrapheap; only out of the ruins can anything worthy of the Gospel arise. This is to do far less than justice to the facts; denigration can be carried much, much too far. When everything has been said that can be said about the Church's faults and failings, its enslavement to a dead past, its divisions, its concern for self-preservation and its pettifogging preoccupation with trivialities, it remains true that up and down the country, in cities, towns and villages, tens of thousands of dedicated men and women, both clerical and lay, bear witness to their faith and seek to serve their fellows in Christ's name in and through the institutional forms they have inherited. Sometimes—and all too often—the Church is woefully weak, presenting little more than a façade, bankrupt of spiritual power. Elsewhere it is just holding its own, grimly hanging on through the loyal devotion of a handful of people. In not a few places it is making forays into the world, winning converts and equipping them for effective Christian witness. Here and there a real dent is made in the line where a congregation is fully and imaginatively committed to mission. Nor should we underrate the immense contribution that is being made to the community by men and women who are seriously trying to relate their faith to their everyday work and life. What, for example, would be the state of voluntary agencies of all kinds without Christian inspiration and leadership? This host of dedicated people, inspired and nurtured by the Church as it is, are the salt of the earth.

We should not, therefore, too easily write off the Church we have inherited as a moribund institution, destined to die a slow and lingering death. Wherever men and women are committed to one another in the name of Christ, there he is and there he is at work. The Church even at its weakest is the Body of Christ, the community in which he chooses to be incarnate, and because of that 'the powers of death shall not prevail against it'.[1] Within the old structures a continuing ministry will have to be exercised for a long time to come. The weakest churches—those I have described as having a mere façade—will probably die out; and that will be no loss. But where traditional congregations of any denomination display real vitality they will go on exercising considerable influence in the communities in which they are located.

Why then do I speak of all this as a holding operation? It is because I believe that a Maginot mentality dominates the life of the Church even at its best; or if the imagery of the Maginot line, behind which the French considered themselves defensively secure at the outbreak of the Second World War, is too extreme, at least we may talk of a fortress mentality: the idea of the Church as a citadel in an alien land from which attacks are launched to enlarge the periphery and bring a few more people into the Christian orbit. Although there are individuals and groups who have rejected this framework of thinking, the main impression of the Church is one of innate conservatism; for the most part the tendency is inward and backward looking, in spite of all the talk of mission and evangelism. Reaction to experiment and adventure is hesitant and fearful. In times of uncertainty and change, much the easiest option is to look for the renewal of the familiar rather than to strike out into uncharted territory. But if the Church is really to be renewed and fulfil its mission in the world, a breakthrough of the existing structure is absolutely necessary; and that is more likely to happen at certain strategic points, where significant advance can be exploited.

This demands an outlook that is foreign to most of those caught up in the traditional structures. It means forsaking altogether the model of the fortress and turning their backs on the idea of an established institution remaining much the same from generation to generation in the midst of a changing world. It means taking seriously the biblical imagery of the people of God on the move. This was the theme of a remarkable sermon preached by Canon John Taylor at the invitation of the Baptist Missionary Society.[2] He expounded the theme that since the days of Constantine the Church has generally thought of itself in terms of a settled community, establishing little Christendoms, when Christendom as such had disappeared. By contrast, the Bible begins with the story of a nomadic people, with Abraham leaving Haran, going out 'not knowing where he was to go'.[3] It is continued in Exodus, when Moses led a band of slaves into the wilderness, forsaking the fleshpots of Egypt. After long years of settlement in Canaan, the exile in Babylon was a catastrophic reminder of Israel's true destiny, dependent on God, and not on the false security of the political and religious establishment in Jerusalem. 'The Son of man has nowhere to lay his head',[4] and his disciples were scattered abroad throughout the Mediterranean world, preaching the Gospel. In the first three centuries of the Christian era there were no church buildings, meetings for worship and mutual encouragement taking place in private houses, and institutionalization being at a minimum. All this was changed with the conversion of Constantine and the advent of *pax christiana*, though the nomadic emphasis was kept alive in the wanderings of the friars and the recurring missionary movements. But the periods of greatest expansion have coincided with the times when Christians were on the move, as in the apostolic age and the century and a half of mission in Asia and Africa following the lead of such pioneers as William Carey and Adoniram Judson.

This same spirit and outlook, Canon Taylor maintained, has now to be recaptured by the Church in the modern world. Christians are again being summoned to be the people of God, scattered abroad everywhere, witnessing to their Faith and forsaking the security of their little Christendoms. The model is the nomadic people, not the settled community. The response to the 'God who summons man into the future is always one of faith, of venturing into an area of which we have no maps'.[5] But when all this has been said, we have to recognize that the spirit of adventure will at first animate only a small minority; the great majority, wedded to the inheritance of the past, will opt for the safe and the familiar; they will not be prepared to go out not knowing where they are going. The breakthroughs, as I have called them, will have to occur at strategic points and then be exploited.

Already there are signs that a start has begun to be made. Its background lies in the growing co-operation made possible by the establishment of Councils of Churches in various parts of the country, leading in some instances to the development of group and team ministries; but a new impetus was given to adventurous pioneering by the resolution adopted at the Nottingham Faith and Order Conference in 1964, calling on the Churches 'to designate areas of ecumenical experiment, at the request of local congregations or in new towns and housing areas. In such cases', it was resolved, 'there should be experiment in ecumenical group ministries, in sharing buildings and in the development of mission.'[6] This decision was a clear declaration of intent to put into effect at the grass roots the recommendation of the Lund Conference of 1952 that the Churches should 'act together in all matters, except those in which deep differences of conviction compel them to act separately'.[7]

The first tentative steps taken thus far are summarized by Robert Jeffery in a survey of 170 experiments either in progress or in process of being planned.[8] Most of them go little further than the sharing of buildings in co-operative activity between churches of different denominations. Anything like real integration is very rare and still exploratory. Jeffery cites three examples of particular significance: in the town of Desborough in Northamptonshire, on the housing estate of Blackbird Leys on the outskirts of Oxford, and in a new development area at Corby, also in Northamptonshire.

The Desborough experiment began with the growing co-operation of the clergy and ministers of the four Churches (Anglican, Methodist, Congregational and Baptist) in this little town of about 5000 inhabitants. The exchange of pulpits and united services on special occasions, together with the inauguration of a twenty-four-hour vigil for unity, in which the local Roman Catholics subsequently joined, led to the formation of a Council of Churches in 1963, as a result of which a mission to the whole town was planned. 'Project '65' as it was called, involved Christians of all four Churches meeting one another in house groups and beginning to learn that they belonged together in the faith they professed. Although this first concerted effort failed to touch more than the fringe of the uncommitted in the community, it did mean that the lay people had discovered one another in Christ, and there was no going back on this newly found partnership in mission. The possibility of one Church in Desborough was now an inescapable goal, and it was natural that after the Nottingham Conference the town should ask to be designated the first area of ecumenical experiment.

No attempt has been made to rush the fences, everyone concerned realizing that the Churches had to grow together step by step. To that end nine commissions were appointed to deal with (1) the ministry, (2) children's and youth work, (3) clubs, societies and organizations, (4) publications, (5) buildings and land, (6) liturgy, worship and church design, (7) outreach and service, (8) church order, discipline and finance, and (9) links with denominations. Each commission was composed of members of all four congregations, five under the leadership of lay people and numbers 1, 6, 8 and 9 chaired by the vicar and ministers of the Free Churches respectively. Those involved have been conscious that progress might necessarily be slow, if solid foundations were to be laid. To quote a writer in the parish magazine: 'How long this "engagement" will last will depend upon the progress in the commissions, the breakdown of natural fear and resistance, and the faith and will of the Church to be obedient to the Will of God. This took the Church in South India over twenty years to achieve, it may well take us as long, but the time it takes is nothing like so important as the direction it takes.'[9] Now, at the time of writing, the announcement has been made that the Anglican and Methodist churches have agreed to enter into full partnership; the parish church will be used for all services and the Methodist property sold, the proceeds going to rebuild the parish hall as a community centre.

Blackbird Leys is an experiment of an entirely different kind. Here on this new housing estate, a priest-missioner of the Anglican Church had been at work for four years when the Oxford Council of Churches proposed that it should be designated an area of ecumenical experiment. This was made possible by the readiness of the Congregationalists, with the support of the other Free Churches, to appoint and house a minister on the estate to work in close collaboration with the priest-missioner in the newly built Church of the Holy Family. The Bishop of Oxford, whose consent to the project had first to be secured, was prepared to give his blessing to it, with certain provisos, the most important of which were that there should be separately advertised Anglican and Free Church services and that the question of intercommunion would have to be governed by the regulations of the Church of England in force at the time.[10] However, there was to be the maximum co-operation in service to the community, and the whole venture was to be guided by a parish meeting, with the Chairman and Treasurer appointed irrespective of denomination. This, of course, falls short of one church on the estate, but it goes a very long way towards it.

The plan for Corby New Town contains the most far-reaching proposals of all. As in Desborough, the initiative has come from Anglicans, Methodists, Congregationalists and Baptists who formed a study group to consider the way in which the Nottingham resolution could be fully implemented in a new development area. They presented their report to representatives of the participating denominations in Northamptonshire on 1 March 1967, and authorization was given for its publication.[11] It is an impressive document which deserves careful consideration by all those planning united action for mission in any locality. The members of the group declared their conviction 'that the Churches could no longer afford—either in money, manpower or on grounds of scandal—to act independently in newly developing areas. Just as industry and secular government want to deal with "the Church" and not with many churches so we believe that people making a new life in a new area want to face one call and not many. Our basic assumption has therefore been that we must make suggestions for a single Christian congregation with one main centre, sponsored by several (we would hope all) of the major denominations.'[12]

Taking this as its premise, the study group proposes one membership, consisting of all those moving into the district in good standing with their respective Churches and the admission of others through baptism either by immersion or affusion, the venture to be under the leadership of a mixed team consisting in the first instance of at least two ordained ministers of different denominations and including laymen as well. One of the more imaginative ideas is that certain ordained members of the team might be in secular employment, whereby, besides other advantages, 'the assumption that the ministry of word and sacraments is essentially a full-time professional occupation could be counteracted.'[13] Eucharistic worship, balancing both word and sacrament, would be at the heart of the church's life, and full intercommunion would be guaranteed from the outset. 'We considered the possibility of separate celebrations of the Eucharist by the different traditions within the experiment but felt bound to reject it because (a) it would divide the congregation during the period of early growth, when unity is essential, and (b) if the habit took root it could prove difficult to terminate.'[14] The entire project is firmly oriented towards mission and the involvement of the whole congregation in the life of the community. With that in view, a simple and flexible building is envisaged, at least for the first five years, while the venture is getting under way and experience is being gained. It is further proposed that a sponsoring body, representing all the denominations concerned, should have oversight in initiating the experiment, in making the first appointments to the team and in continuing consultation with them, in arranging the necessary financial support with the denominational authorities, in giving guidance in matters of theology and discipline, and in reporting to the participating Churches and the British Council of Churches.

How far all this is going to be implemented remains to be seen. But here at any rate is a breakthrough in thinking and a blueprint for constructive action. Corby could well be the pioneer project for many development areas in new towns and housing estates, and it will be watched with the greatest interest. What cannot be doubted is this: the Church cannot afford to play safe and miss the opportunity that experiments of this kind provide. As the authors of the report say, 'We believe that ecumenical action must be made local in mission and unity and that therefore it is in these new towns that the key battle is to be won in the 1970s.'[15]

Robert Jeffery's survey of areas of ecumenical experiment is by no means exhaustive of all that is happening up and down the country, offering promise of a significant breakthrough of the inherited structures of the Church. Two further examples are of particular interest.

The first of these is described by Neville Cryer and Ernest Goodridge in their account of the growth of ecumenical co-operation in Addiscombe, a typical outer London suburb in the neighbourhood of Croydon.[16] In this predominantly dormitory district, populated largely by commuters to the City, the churches have a history of ecumenical co-operation dating back to the immediate post-war years. I myself was privileged to share in a united mission to the whole community in 1949, sponsored by the Anglicans, Methodists and Congregationalists, and I was impressed at the time by the mutual trust and confidence already obtaining between the clergy and ministers and by the way in which this was growing amongst the members of their respective congregations.

However, this was still no more than co-operation between the churches in a joint enterprise: a state of affairs which is happily now being taken for granted in a good many other places. It was with the appointment of Neville Cryer as Vicar of St Mary Magdalene in 1963 and the subsequent arrival of Ernest Goodridge to take charge of the nearby Methodist church that a new pattern of mission to suburbia became possible. The story is told in full in their account of what has so far been achieved and of the frustrations and disappointments they encountered. Here was an attempt to bring together strong, established congregations of different denominations, with a long history in separation behind them, into one church renewed for mission.

Just as Rome was not built in a day, so those who have pioneered this venture have found that everything cannot be achieved at once, even against a background of growing co-operation over the years. The focus of the experiment has been the relationship between St Mary's and Addiscombe

Methodist church. They still fall short of being one congregation, but their worship, their organizations and their evangelistic and social outreach have been progressively integrated under the leadership of a team ministry. Other churches in the neighbourhood have become more or less closely related to this spearhead, and the story is one of pooling more and more resources in service to the community. Particularly encouraging has been the deepening relationship with the Roman Catholics, though some congregations of a conservative evangelical outlook have felt compelled to stand aloof.

The importance of what has been happening at Addiscombe is that it illustrates the problems confronting the Church if it is to break through in ministry to the whole community in an area where it is already strongly established in the old patterns. There is no possibility of starting entirely *de novo* or of exploring a radically new approach, as in the example to which I shall be referring next. Of necessity, the basis for renewal is in the old structures, which have to be put together piece by piece, discarding the useless and adapting the serviceable to a fresh purpose. It is rather like building a new house out of materials taken from old ones with an admixture of modern equipment. Thus in the nature of the case a breakthrough, when it occurs, will not be startling or dramatic; it will be the beginning of a process which will have to be gradually and painstakingly exploited. The goal of one Church united in mission to the community will be an ideal towards which there can be steady progress, once the resolve has been made by even a few—in the first instance in Addiscombe by an Anglican priest and a Methodist minister—to work together to that end. The resolve, translated into action, is the initial breakthrough.

The second example is what is known as the 'Thamesmead Christian Community'. This is an attempt to plan a concerted approach to a new development area within the jurisdiction of the Greater London Authority, on the borders of Woolwich and Erith. Over the next few years 60,000 families are to be housed on reclaimed marshland, and already at the time of writing the first families are moving into their new homes. Largely through the initiative of the Bishop of Woolwich, a consultation was arranged between representatives of all the major denominations, and a project committee was formed to draw up a scheme for common buildings serviced by an ecumenical team ministry. Initially it was hoped that all religious bodies would at least agree to use the same premises and avoid any denominational expenditure on bricks and mortar. However, approaches to the extreme evangelical groups proved abortive because they declared that they could not co-operate in an ecumenical venture in any way, and the Baptists and the Roman Catholics resolved to build their own churches, although they were prepared to share in the use of the ecumenical building envisaged for the town centre. When it came to the crunch, the project was largely left in the hands of the Anglicans, the Congregationalists, the Methodists and the Presbyterians, all of whom promised not to erect denominational premises, to share in a united ministry, and to underwrite the expenses for a two-year period of a project secretary seconded with salary by the Anglicans.[17]

The committee began by envisaging a central building located within the main shopping area, with the William Temple Anglican church on the adjoining Abbey Estate and two pastoral units situated at strategic points serving as outposts. The ecumenical centre was to comprise a church seating 150 people, an adjoining hall with movable partitions capable of accommodating varying numbers of up to 500, a kitchen, a restaurant, offices and cubicle bedrooms for students on short courses. The pastoral units were to be of simple design, providing homes for two of the ministerial members of the team divided by a small meeting place, kitchen, coffee bar and offices. The ministers assigned to a pastoral unit were to have responsibility for the people living in their immediate neighbourhood, irrespective of former denominational allegiance, while a variety of services of worship were to be held in the centre and at the outlying stations. All other forms of ministry in the community were to be fully integrated. Pending the erection of these premises and the appointment of the complete team, a start was to be made by using the William Temple Anglican church as a base, where a monthly Free Church service was already being held, conducted by the Presbyterian minister and the Congregational woman lay pastor who had special responsibility for developments in Thamesmead.

In the event the scheme had to be modified, at least for the time being. As I have indicated, the Baptists felt unable to commit themselves to such comprehensive co-operation and announced their intention of building churches of their own in two of the outlying districts. Accordingly the committee has abandoned the idea of a pastoral unit in the neighbourhood where the first of these churches is to be erected. It is hoped, however, that the Baptist minister, just appointed, will collaborate with the work of the ecumenical centre and that in the course of time there will be a growing together leading to a really fruitful relationship.

Roman Catholic involvement has gone as far as it can at the present juncture. Taking advantage of the new ecumenical outlook following the Second Vatican Council, the Roman Catholic authorities have been closely connected with the Thamesmead project, and, although feeling compelled to erect their own church buildings, they are committed to maximum possible collaboration in the activities of the ecumenical centre. In any case, the number of those expected to attend Mass compared with anticipated Protestant figures would necessitate much larger buildings than the ecumenical project is able to envisage. In other words Roman Catholic involvement is as complete as circumstances allow.

Apart from the difficulties encountered in securing the full co-operation of all the Churches in the Thamesmead project, the scheme has had to be modified to some extent by financial considerations. In the early stages, building is to be confined to the ecumenical centre and one pastoral unit, though this does not preclude expansion later on: planning is to be determined not by a blueprint for buildings but in the light of the growth of Thamesmead as a community. For the time being also the idea of a fully integrated team ministry has had to be replaced by a group ministry of those appointed by the four co-operating denominations. This falls short of one varied ministry to the community, irrespective of denomination, and means its provisional replacement by the co-operation of ministers of different denominations who still retain something of their specific responsibility to separate congregations, however closely these congregations work together. Nevertheless it is a great step forward to ensure a common use of buildings by Anglicans, Congregationalists, Methodists and Presbyterians and an integrated plan of action which can lead to further advance.

The Thamesmead project is instructive for the frustrations

it has encountered no less than for the considerable progress it has been able to achieve. From the standpoint of many Baptists it is nothing short of tragic that the London Baptist Association and its North Kent group of churches should have resolved not to enter into the full degree of commitment and to maintain their own separate existence after the old pattern. Here was an imaginative proposal for a real breakthrough, at the very least in terms of a common use of buildings; but scarce resources are again being allowed to be prodigally expended because it is supposed that this is necessary for maintaining a specific evangelical witness. The question has to be pressed, 'Why must this be done in isolation in a separate building?' It suggests the fortress mentality to which I have earlier referred and an attachment to patterns of church life which are increasingly irrelevant to the present day. Here is an opportunity to break free from the shackles, and it is being lost.

These are harsh words, but they are written by a Baptist with a very troubled conscience in the knowledge that there are many others who share his sense of deep disturbance. I know there is another side to the question. It can be argued that the same strictures should be applied to Roman Catholics and to all the sects who have refused to co-operate at all. As long as there are profound theological differences, separation is inevitable; and the more strongly these differences are emphasized, the more persuasive will be the case for independent action. In the present situation is not an evangelical centre a necessary complement to an ecumenical project such as that conceived for Thamesmead?

At first sight it may appear that I have unfairly discriminated against my fellow Baptists as compared with the

Roman Catholics whom I have not criticized in the same way for deciding to erect their own buildings. But the two cases are not parallel. While it is to be regretted that the Roman Catholics feel they must have their own schools and places of worship and not utilize common premises, we have to take into account the practical difficulties involved as well as the ecclesiastical tradition in which they stand. After all, the degree of their commitment to the Thamesmead project is striking evidence of the enormous strides they have taken recently in ecumenical co-operation. They are proposing to engage in the venture as far as they possibly can, and the door is wide open to creative growth in the future. With the Baptists it is different. There is nothing forward looking about their decision; it is hanging on to the old ways, in spite of the fact that in other places, like Desborough and Corby, Baptists are to be found in the forefront of the ecumenical venture. It reflects that element in Baptist life which is suspicious of all ecumenical involvement and tends in a sectarian and exclusivist direction. While the sects will be found everywhere insisting on preserving the purity of their doctrine as they understand it, it is a sad thing that one of the major denominations, many of whose members have taken a prominent part in the ecumenical movement, should fail at so crucial a moment to measure up to this new opportunity.

Despite all the difficulties and frustrations, the Thamesmead Project does hold out hope for a flexible and imaginative approach in a development area. The fact that four denominations have committed themselves to this degree of co-operation and are ready to experiment with new forms of ministry adapted to a rapidly changing situation is a beacon light of encouragement to others elsewhere. The limited plans to be put into operation in the early stages are open-ended and offer promise of exploitation as the situation develops. In course of time some of those who do not feel able to become fully involved at this juncture may yet do so. At any rate it is important that the doors should be left wide open and the spirit of adventure kept alive.

Not all the instances of breakthrough at the grass roots are ecumenical in origin. Some are initiated by churches of a particular denomination, though they have implications beyond the denomination concerned and point the way forward to ecumenical action. I select three examples from very different situations.

The first of these is in a rural district of Lincolnshire, where fifteen village churches of the Anglican Communion have been brought together under a group ministry.[18] This has come about partly through the pressure of sheer hard facts and partly through the realization that a new approach has to be made to ministry in the countryside. For generations it has been assumed that every village should have its own parish church, with its own incumbent, and this has been ideally seen as the centre of the life of the community. Unhappily ideal and reality have more often than not proved to be far apart. The process of secularization has not been confined to the large urban areas and, with the drift of population from the country to the towns and the advent of modern transport, the village has ceased to be the self-contained community that once it was. Moreover, the rift between church and chapel has long been a deeply divisive factor in rural areas, not infrequently crystallized in the hostility of prominent families.

As yet very little, if anything, has been done to tackle this latter problem; the ecumenical movement has scarcely touched the countryside. But at least there are signs here and there of the breakdown of Anglican isolationism; an almost inevitable corollary of the parson's freehold in every village. The hard fact is that there are simply not enough clergy to man all the parishes, and the number of vacant livings is increasing all the time. What appears to be a calamity to those wedded to the old pattern has been seen by others as an opportunity for a breakthrough to a more imaginative and relevant Christian ministry.

This is what has happened in the Lincolnshire area of South Ormsby. In 1949 the bishop invited the vicar of this small parish to take responsibility for a group ministry to serve fourteen other parishes, previously served by six elderly and independent incumbents. Not all the livings were vacant at the time; a start had to be made with eight, and a curate was straightway appointed to assist the vicar. Over the subsequent years the remaining churches have come into the scheme and an additional curate and deaconess have been recruited to make up the team.

Welding so many tiny, scattered congregations into one community has been an immense task, calling for imagination and great perseverance. The South Ormsby experiment was an ambitious attempt to break new ground, and it has shown the way for similar ventures in other parts of the countryside.[19] But it is only a beginning. As we have seen, the rift in village life still remains; church and chapel are as far apart as ever; a large proportion of the rural population remains alienated from the traditional structures; the idea of one Church united for mission is a concept that has scarcely been entertained by the vast majority of Christians who live outside the urban areas. If we can see the signs of a breakthrough in places like South Ormsby, it is only the very thin edge of the wedge. To exploit it is a mammoth operation.

The second experiment is of a very different kind; so different in fact, as to be almost antithetical to the one just described. When Ernest Southcott, now Provost of Southwark Cathedral, was vicar of Halton in Leeds, he came to the conclusion that the Church could effectively exercise its ministry only when it was prepared to break out of the walls of its buildings and become identified with people where they actually live and work. He, therefore, developed the idea of the house-church, going back to the practice of apostolic times when Christians had no ecclesiastical buildings of their own and met for worship and fellowship in one another's homes. 'Two particular theological pressures', he wrote, 'have brought about the house-church: one to connect Baptism and Communion, membership and worship, and the other to connect the two communities, the congregation and the parish. We have seen that Baptism for the many and Communion for the few is a contradiction in terms . . . If people won't come to the Parish Communion to see the point of it, we must take Communion to them.'[20] Little imagination is required to appreciate the new dimension of significance that this affords to the prayer of humble access when it is offered in the kitchen rather than at the altar: 'We do not presume to come to this Thy table, trusting in our own righteousness . . .' Home and Church are thus manifestly one. 'In the homes in Halton people have said, "I *see* now that I can worship God in my working clothes." "I *see* my house as part of God's world now." '[21]

Two kinds of house meeting evolved from the early beginnings: the gathering of regular worshippers in Christian homes—what Southcott calls the 'parish meeting in dispersion'—and meetings with or without celebrations in the homes of non-church-goers: the 'intensive house-church' and the 'extensive house-church'. The target was ultimately to have such gatherings in every street in the parish. The result of all this was to expose the Church in action to many people who would not otherwise have seen it as anything more than an esoteric exercise within a somewhat forbidding building. Furthermore the ecumenical implications were inescapable; for Anglicans inevitably discovered their Roman Catholic and Free Church neighbours in a fresh light. 'In the house-church we are all near enough to our fellow Christians of other denominations to meet in a new and vital way.'[22] Barriers were broken down that hitherto had seemed insurmountable.

Ernest Southcott's experiment with the house-church is important not only because it illustrates a *breakthrough* of barriers separating Christians from one another and from the rest of the community, but also because it emphasizes the need for a *breakdown* of the large and frequently impersonal congregation where most folk cannot really find one another. 'The Christian cell', says Southcott, 'is formed of not more than twelve people.'[23] This has been a continuing theme of Canon John Taylor in the newsletters he has written for the Church Missionary Society. Taylor believes that the future of the Christian mission everywhere lies in small cells of committed men and women, the dispersion, scattered abroad throughout the world bearing witness to their faith.[24]

The suggestion that we need to look to the breakdown of the Church into small intimate fellowships appears to be in direct antithesis to the development of group ministries such as that pioneered at South Ormsby. The one emphasizes the need for a breakdown of congregational and parish structures into small units; the other illustrates the desirability of bringing weak and scattered communities together. In actual fact the two experiments are complementary. Rationalization of structure, the better deployment of ministry and the encouragement of wider community should go hand in hand with the formation within that context of small effective Christian cells. In any case there is no simple blueprint for the reformation of church structures, no universal panacea which can be applied to all situations. Breakthroughs will be piecemeal and varied, and their exploitation will consist in stimulating new patterns of mission on a wider front. This will happen as one experiment sparks off another, and the insights gained contribute to further advance. The house-church and the Christian cell are obviously of crucial importance in this respect.

The third example is the Notting Hill group ministry and the ecumenical centre which arose out of it. Following the race riots in 1958, Lord Soper proposed that the Methodists should explore a new approach to mission in the area, taking seriously the social problems which the community was facing. Accordingly a team of three ministers was brought together: one responsible for the worship of the Church, one concerned with race relations and the third with social welfare. The imaginative way in which Geoffrey Ainger and his colleagues set about their formidable task brought not only new life to the church, but also new hope to the community.

Out of this initially Methodist enterprise, the Notting Hill ecumenical centre was born, housed in another Methodist building which would otherwise have become redundant. Under the chairmanship of the Bishop of Kensington, this is not simply a co-operative venture in which Anglicans, Roman Catholics and Free Churchmen are sharing; it is ecumenical in the much wider sense that it is concerned with the whole community and the relationships which affect it, stretching far beyond its borders. It is taking seriously the basic meaning of *oikumene* as designating the entire inhabited world.

To quote from its own declared purpose:

> The Centre grew out of the urgent need to provide encounter between people who are willing to learn from each other and seek to provide relevant ways in which they can effectively engage life on all levels . . . From the grass roots level the Church seeks the total well-being of the neighbourhood, both in terms of its own needs as well as its active participation in the wider problems of the world community.[25]

Here Christian and non-Christian meet in an open situation where dialogue is possible, common concerns explored and relevant action initiated.

The programme of the centre covers consultations on such subjects as 'The Care of the Dying', 'Unattached Teenagers', 'Immigrants in Industry' and 'Mental Health'; it provides a programme of education in theological, urban and moral problems; it has brought together writers, artists and social workers to encourage the cultural development of the community; and it has initiated action on housing and world poverty.

Those most directly concerned with the centre would not claim that they have done more than take the first tentative steps in exploring what ecumenical action in the fullest sense really means. But they have made a start in a singularly challenging situation, and what they are able to achieve will have significance far beyond the bounds of Notting Hill.

Four major difficulties or objections are likely to be encountered in the proposal to proliferate such experiments as these at the grass roots.

1. The first is the legal problem. This is not so intractable as far as new development areas are concerned, where no church is yet in existence. Here there is more flexibility and room for manoeuvre, though the problem is still a considerable one since churches resolved to engage in ecumenical experiments are restricted by the legal requirements of the denominations to which they belong. But the difficulties abound where the Church is already established. Reference has already been made to the Church of England with its ties to the State, its responsibility, in theory at any rate, for providing pastoral care for the whole population, its parochial organization based on the parson's freehold and its outdated system of patronage. The Free Churches are no less bound by their trust deeds, precluding the use of their premises for other than denominational purposes, and in many cases subject to the decisions of a local congregation. Nothing can be done to produce a more fluid state of affairs without comprehensive legislation, but some of this is already under consideration or in the pipeline. The measure now before the Houses of Parliament permitting the sharing of churches with the approval of denominational authorities should, if passed, go a long way towards freeing local groups of Christians to implement a more rational use of resources. Again, the Fenton–Morley Report contains proposals for dealing with the anomalies of the parson's freehold and the system of patronage by providing for a Central Ministry Commission and Diocesan Ministry

Commissions to facilitate a complete redeployment of the clergy by bringing appointments to benefices under planned control. How far these latter proposals will be adopted remains to be seen, and they have already encountered some of the conservative opposition of entrenched interests. But at least the Churches have awoken to the urgent need for action, and it should not be beyond the wit of man, given the resolve, to loosen some of the knots and liberate the Church from its legal bondage. This is not the most difficult hurdle to surmount.

2. Perhaps the biggest fear in the minds of many people, particularly those in positions of responsibility, is that the proliferation of ecumenical experiments of the kind outlined will lead to the emergence of a new denomination or new denominations, calculated to bring about even further divisiveness than we have at present. If local ventures anticipate agreement at the regional, national or even international levels, the result will be anarchy. Let union between the Churches become an accomplished fact and then implement it at the grass roots. Jumping the gun will only make negotiations between the denominations more difficult, and scare off many who would otherwise be ready to become involved. It is a policy of disastrously short-circuiting most of the important issues.

While this view is widely held, I believe it to be profoundly mistaken. For one thing it tends, as I have already suggested, to overemphasize the importance of conciliar agreement at the expense of actual working concord at the grass roots. But the basic error is one of strategy. Ecclesiastical negotiations are inevitably cumbersome and slow. They need the pilot projects to point the way ahead and show by their mistakes as well as by their successes what can be achieved on a larger front. Without the pioneers, the ecumenical movement may cease to be a movement at all, and grind to a halt in a mass of documents and endless talk. To avoid this danger the Churches as a whole through their representative leaders must encourage experiments wherever they are being made, even if they lead to anomalies; and there are heartening signs, as in Northamptonshire, that this is increasingly being recognized.

After all, those who are committed to ecumenical action are dedicated to the goal of one Church. They are not separatists. There is all the difference in the world between those of sect-like mentality who hive off from their fellow Christians and form an exclusive coterie to propagate their own distinctive beliefs and those who, while loyal to the traditions in which they stand and maintaining their roots in them, seek under the impulse of the Spirit to bring together the scattered fragments of the one Church into a visible fellowship where they live and work.

This involves both patience and discipline on the part of those engaged in such ecumenical experiments. It is no easy road for hot-headed enthusiasts; the wreckage of disappointment lies ahead for all those who are unprepared to face the difficulties on the way or who try to brush uncomfortable issues under the carpet. The projects described above amply illustrate the need for careful planning and continuing consultation with the Church authorities concerned. The Desborough experiment, in particular, underlines the crucial importance of building mutual trust between clergy, ministers and lay people, and this may be a long process of growing together. But relations of confidence between those actually involved at the grass roots and their parent bodies are no less vital. Otherwise the new branches may break loose from the stem and wither away. The significance of ecumenical experiments would be lost if they were seen as separate growths, freak plants destined to flourish for a while and then die out. They must be organic to the life of the whole Church, the evidence of new flowering from the old roots.

3. This brings us to the vexed question of intercommunion. We have already noted that the study group concerned with Corby New Town has declared that it cannot recommend anything short of full eucharistic fellowship from the outset of the experiment. This poses no problem here or anywhere else for the Free Churches, who for the most part have welcomed all Christian believers to their celebrations, irrespective of ecclesiastical allegiance. With the Anglicans, Orthodox and Romans it is different. Their traditional position has been to maintain an inseparable connexion between an episcopally ordained ministry and a valid administration of the Eucharist. Hence to receive communion at the hands of a Free Church minister would be to receive less than Christ himself. As for the admission to the Sacrament of anyone across the barriers of those Churches with an episcopally ordained ministry, still more of those without it, this has been resisted on the ground that membership within a visibly united Church is indispensable before common participation in sacramental worship can be regarded as permissible; though exceptions to the rule are sometimes allowed for under special circumstances. The suggestion that intercommunion should be the road to organic unity has been met with the contention that it is rightly understood as the expression of unity, not the means to it.

Over the past few years the situation has been changing

rapidly. As Christians have come to know one another, to trust one another and to co-operate with one another across the ecclesiastical frontiers, it makes less and less sense to them to be told that they may not unite in sacramental communion. In the words of one of my own colleagues, 'when you have come to share the Faith in depth with other Christians, it is intolerable not to join with them in the Eucharist.' This sort of experience is leading to more and more occasions of intercommunion and the old rules are becoming increasingly difficult to commend.

The report recently published by the Commission appointed by the Archbishops of Canterbury and York under the chairmanship of the Bishop of Bristol recognizes the changed situation and makes a number of recommendations.[26] Amongst other suggestions, it proposes that Anglican celebration should be open to those of other persuasions 'where local congregations or other groups of Christians are meeting together either in sustained efforts or on special occasions to promote the unity, ministry or mission of the Church'.[27] A majority were in favour of reciprocal intercommunion under the same circumstances, 'so long as the Churches concerned are in relationships of friendship and mutual acknowledgment with the Church of England',[28] but a minority dissented on the ground that the achievement of unity within the historic episcopate is a necessary precondition of mutual sacramental participation.[29]

How this report will be received by the Convocations and the Church Assembly (or the General Synod) remains to be seen at the time of writing. While it goes a long way towards opening the doors and windows, it is questionable whether the majority of recommendations go quite as far as is necessary to permit the kind of eucharistic fellowship envisaged at Corby. If they are in any way weakened, the scope of ecumenical experiments elsewhere would be seriously limited. Of course, there will be those who in conscience feel that they cannot share in reciprocal intercommunion, even in such special circumstances; but I do not believe that such a position can much longer be embodied in rules inhibiting others. In many places the lid is coming off the cauldron, and it is patently evident that clergy and lay people alike will not accept a disciplinary decree which they believe to be out of touch with the realities of the situation.

This is being amply demonstrated in the reaction to the papal encyclical on birth control. The ferment in the Roman Church extends far beyond the particular issue in question. It is a crisis of authority. No longer can it be assumed in this most authoritarian of all Churches that the rank and file will meekly submit to every *Diktat* from above. How all this is going to work out no one can tell, but the lesson is clear to read. Authority must commend itself as wise and sensitive to the realities of the situation if it is to be respected; and the relevance of this to the question of intercommunion is plain. The facts must be faced and the regulations be made flexible enough to take into account what is actually happening at the local level.

As I have already indicated, many in the episcopal tradition will find the greatest difficulty in accepting such a conclusion; and their consciences must be respected. But as Christians get to know one another and face what God has undoubtedly been doing through their respective traditions, it becomes increasingly difficult to maintain that he has used one order of ministry rather than another, still less that he restricts his sacramental self-giving to celebrations by the episcopally ordained. The facts belie it. As a Roman Catholic put it at a recent ecumenical conference, 'When a Free Church minister celebrates Holy Communion, does God give his people a stone?' Faced with the question in these stark terms, it is very difficult to go on talking about the validity or otherwise of the administration of the sacraments by Christians of other traditions. The debate resolves itself into one about the proper ordering of the Church. But, unless I am very blind, that removes one of the basic objections to intercommunion that has so often been advanced. The issue is one of church order and discipline, not of the validity of sacramental observance.

4. I have touched on three issues which affect the implementation of ecumenical experiments at the grass roots and which in different degrees and in different places are likely to inhibit any rapid breakthrough of the existing structures: the legal jungle, the fear of further division and the problem of intercommunion in advance of organic unity. But by far the biggest obstacle is people: ordinary men and women in all their variety, idiosyncrasy and limitations. Some of the discussions about the renewal of the Church appear to assume that every Christian is a potential pioneer and that once the pioneering spirit has been awakened there will be broad agreement on what needs to be done. This has only to be stated to be seen to be a travesty of the facts. In every congregation, whatever the denomination, there is a relatively small nucleus of potential leaders; most of the committed members are those who are in need of pastoral care and feel they have little to contribute to the Church's mission other than quiet and steady support, the importance of which is by no means to be minimized; while there is generally a large fringe of adherents who receive far more than they are

ready to give. This mixed company constitutes the average congregation. Is it realistic to expect of them a united and whole-hearted response to the call to adventurous mission? As someone remarked about a meeting convened for 'Christian Action' and attended by a predominantly elderly audience, 'It is cruel to ask all these old people to act!'

The reaction to the facts of the situation—particularly on the conservative Evangelical wing—is to say that here lies the real trouble with the Church: it is unregenerate. It is not meant to be such a mixed company, but should consist only of the fully committed. Then, and only then, will it be fitted for mission. Those who are inclined to take this line are bound to be more or less exclusive, and their ministry will necessarily be limited to a fraction of the population. Moreover they still face the problem of the mixed congregation, however stringent the conditions for membership. But an inevitable corollary of this attitude is a reluctance to collaborate with Churches which see their mission in inclusive terms and a resolve to continue in independence to preserve their own purity of life and doctrine.

Pioneers in ecumenical experiments everywhere will have to reckon with this type of churchmanship whatever may be its denominational or sectarian label. To suppose that the perfect visible unity of all Christians will be realized under earthly conditions is to cherish an ideal beyond fragmentary achievement, human nature being what it is and given the fact that some will always see their calling in exclusive terms. What is important is that those who are committed to ecumenical adventure should not be prevented or discouraged from going forward because there are congregations within their locality which feel compelled to stand aloof. It is equally important to keep the doors open and the lines of communication in being as far as that is possible. The pattern for doing so is admirably set out in Neville Cryer's and Ernest Goodridge's account of ecumenical co-operation in Addiscombe. 'We believed', they say, 'that New Testament principle and practice required of us respect for Christians more exclusive and legalistic than our own, and we sought to express this by continuing to provide material and information of common interest.'[30] By maintaining openness of this kind 'a fundamental principle of unity' is preserved and the possibility of greater understanding and closer co-operation kept alive.

Leaving aside those congregations which for different reasons are unwilling to share in an ecumenical experiment, it is by no means plain sailing for those who do. Besides the drag of what I have called the mixed community of Christians which makes up any particular expression of the Church, those who belong to the committed nucleus will not always agree or find it easy to collaborate with one another. The process of growing together is a long and sometimes a painful one, as all those who have been involved in such ventures know to their cost. It is a case of what the prophet described as 'here a little, there a little'.[31] But this is the way forward. To repeat and underline the main point I have been making, the crucial breakthroughs will be at the grass roots, where Christians discover one another in the unity of the Faith and in the call to mission. With that in view, the participants in the Nottingham Conference placed on record the following resolution: 'Since unity, mission and renewal are inseparable we invite the member churches to plan jointly so that all in each place may act together forthwith in common mission and service to the world.'[32] Whatever be the frustrations and however stumbling the steps, this is where renewal will come and fresh inspiration be given to the Church at large.

But for that to happen there must be clergy, ministers and lay people prepared to pioneer where they are. I believe that there are many ready to do so if they could see the way ahead. Some of them are to be found within the renewal groups which have sprung up in most of the larger denominations and which at the time of writing are planning to join together in an ecumenical task force, pledged to action at the local level. Their total numerical strength may not be very great as yet, but it could markedly increase, if once it were seen that real progress could be made. The project 'People Next Door', organized by the British Council of Churches and the Conference of British Missionary Societies in 1967 introduced Christians in many places to the possibilities of co-operative action and began to widen their horizons. However much entrenched conservatism there may be, we should not underestimate the considerable resources of potentially dedicated men and women which remain largely untapped because they see nothing really to inspire them. And if this is true of the laity, it is no less true of those ordained to the ministry. A former priest in the archdiocese of Westminster and now a Roman Catholic layman speaks for many in a review in *New Christian* when he writes:

> The priesthood today is part of a church whose structures are tottering and whose leaders are frightened, yet whose mission is from Christ, as we believe. What is the use of patching it up with breviary reform and such trivialities when the task is to find a ministry capable of serving the Christian church of the future? This is rather vague, I

> know. But it will remain vague until rebellion becomes responsible and organised, calculated to remove all that chokes the work of Christ in his church and to experiment with new forms of Christian belonging.[33]

It is this pioneering of new forms of Christian belonging for which I am persuaded many are now ready.

Chapter Four

The Wider Context

In the last chapter I argued that the renewal of the Church must begin at the grass roots, where people actually live and work. That is the arena of decisive engagement, and unless the breakthrough occurs there, it will not happen anywhere. Local initiative has to point the way ahead and shape the pattern of the Church of the future.

In the long run this is bound to present a radical challenge to the larger ecclesiastical structures as they at present exist, whether at the regional, national or international levels. As we have already seen, they are now to a considerable degree obsolescent, reflecting the situation of an age that is past. To attempt at all costs to perpetuate them in their present form is to settle for anachronistic irrelevance. At this stage, however, it is impossible to predict the shape of things to come; we are simply at the beginning of a transition period with the old landmarks fast disappearing and the territory still to be mapped for the future. All that we can say with any confidence is that the changes that will take place before this century has run its course will be as far-reaching as those which occurred at the time of the Reformation in the sixteenth century.

The argument that the initiative must come from experiments at the grass roots does not mean sounding the death knell of institutionalism and the introduction of anarchy. As Leslie Paul remarks, 'History does not guide us except to say that without institutions bent on shaping and preserving insights or revelations, these would be lost to us.'[1] Let the extreme radicals take note. Nor can the structures of the future involve a completely new start; continuity with the past has to be preserved. But equally it should not be supposed that the way ahead lies in piecing bits of ecclesiastical machinery together, rather like a patchwork quilt. The shape of things to come will need to be determined by the realities of the grass roots situation, reflecting the new life and new forms of Christian belonging which will emerge out of the present confused scene. In the meanwhile, it is essential that the larger regional, national and international structures should become increasingly flexible and adaptable in a rapidly changing situation. Otherwise they will hinder rather than help the process of growth.

For this to happen there will have to be nothing short of a transformation in the attitude of those in positions of responsibility. Hitherto it has been assumed, with considerable justification, that the rank and file have been far behind their leaders both in ecumenical co-operation and in response to the claims of mission in the modern world. Clear evidence of this is to be seen in the dramatic developments that have taken place in a very short space of time on the international front, of which I shall have more to say in what follows; and it remains true that the vast majority of ordinary Christians have not as yet caught up with the statesmen at the helm. But we have begun to see in the last two or three years significant stirrings at the grass roots, not only in church circles, but in society at large. In particular the voice of youth is being heard in a new and challenging way. It is not any longer plain that adventurous leadership is the prerogative of those in official positions, and this implies the need for acute sensitivity to what is being said and done where Christians are making bold experiments to break out of the prison in which they feel themselves incarcerated. Church leaders will now have to listen as they have not been accustomed to listen before. It is within that context that the plea is made for flexibility and adaptability in the major ecclesiastical structures.

The most immediate and urgent problems present themselves in the relationship of denominations nationally. This does not mean that regional and international structures are unimportant or can be ignored. Quite the contrary. Indeed, Colin Williams is almost certainly right in maintaining that regional planning is the key to united action for mission in the kind of society that is now emerging.[2] Unless, however, there are breakthroughs at the national level where denominations confront one another in their separation, little progress is going to be made either regionally or internationally. This is particularly obvious as far as regional structures are concerned, because they inevitably reflect more comprehensive denominational policy. Without changes in national ecclesiastical organization it is difficult to see how very much rationalization can be achieved at the diocesan, district, association and county levels.

But before considering possible ways of breaking through the national structures, something should be said about the international scene. In recent years more progress has been made here than anywhere else. The formation of the World Council of Churches and its steady growth in membership and influence is one of the most encouraging signs of effective Christian co-operation in our time. Since the assembly in New Delhi in 1961 there has been a marked increase in Orthodox participation and the beginning of involvement by certain conservative Evangelical Churches, such as the Pentecostalists. Most significant of all has been the opening of conversations in depth with the Vatican, leading to the establishment of a Joint Working Group and official representation on the Faith and Order Commission. The presence of large numbers of Roman Catholics at Uppsala was clear evidence of a changed climate and new opportunities of ecumenical collaboration, for which credit is due to outstanding leadership in the World Council, no less than to Pope John XXIII. Nor should we fail to note again in this connexion the integration of the World Council of Churches and the International Missionary Council at New Delhi, whereby the Churches everywhere were offered a new perspective of global responsibility.

All of this marks solid achievement for which we may be deeply thankful, and shows what can be done in a relatively short space of time, given the resolve and imaginative leadership. But much further progress will clearly be impossible without genuine growing together at national, regional and local levels. This may be helped or hindered by the emergence to prominence of World Confessional Bodies. One of the principal features of the present international scene is the increasing influence of organizations such as the Baptist World Alliance, the International Congregational Council, the Lutheran World Federation, the World Methodist Council and the World Presbyterian Alliance. The world-wide Anglican Communion, too, now has its permanent secretariat. These organizations have come into being partly to serve as a means of consultation between Churches of the same Faith and Order, partly (particularly in the Baptist case) to strengthen the hands of minority groups in countries where another Church is predominant, and partly to administer relief programmes.

In the latter case there is obviously a danger of overlapping and the need for co-ordination: a function which in large measure is being fulfilled by the Division of Inter-Church Aid, Refugee and World Service at Geneva. The maximum deployment of resources is, of course, the paramount concern, and without these confessional relief agencies much of the money would not be raised. At the same time the multiplication of appeals for the relief of world poverty has to be constantly watched.

The first and second of the objectives (consultation and strengthening minority Churches) are in themselves entirely laudable and calculated to make no insignificant contribution to ecumenical thought and action. But their importance should not be overrated and they should not be pursued to the detriment of more intensive effort on the national front. The number of international conferences grows at an alarming rate, and the same Church officials are often engaged in more and more consultations at all levels. A warning needs to be sounded about the role of the ecclesiastical functionary who spends his life in aeroplanes, trains and cars, travelling from one meeting to another, and in danger of becoming so involved in conferences and committees that he loses touch with the Church at its basic level. Rationing is not only applicable to food in time of war!

However, the point of greatest tension is the way in which these international relations may hinder rather than help the renewal of the Church for mission in different countries. It should be said quite clearly that denominational ties across national frontiers should not be allowed to become obstacles to unity with other Churches where reunion schemes are under consideration. It is the proper role of the larger organization to assist its constituent Churches to fulfil their mission in whatever way God is calling them to do it. They should never be a drag on the wheels. In the years ahead the World Confessional Bodies will have to be sensitive to the possibility of losing their organizational life for the sake of effective Christian mission. They must not become an end in themselves.

We now turn to the really crucial question in regard to breaking through the main ecclesiastical structures: the relationship of national Churches involved in actual mission at the grass roots and the rationalization of their denominational organizations. Considerable progress has been made in recent years by the establishment and growing influence of the British Council of Churches on which all the major non-Roman denominations have been represented. The proliferation of local affiliated Councils of Churches in which Roman Catholics are increasingly participating has enlarged the area of co-operation, and the Churches have now an instrument for ecumenical consultation and action which was denied to them in former times. It has also been encouraging to note that the National Free Church Federal Council which came into being to co-ordinate the work of the Free Churches has recently decided to merge much of its organization with the British Council of Churches, thus avoiding unnecessary administrative overlapping; and conversations have been opened with the Conference of British Missionary Societies to the same end.

All this is a mark of real progress. But the fact remains that these organizations are in the main consultative, and the constituent bodies preserve their own autonomy and freedom of action. The crucial breakthrough depends on changed denominational structures which will encourage rather than inhibit ecumenical renewal at the fundamental level; and here the obstacles are formidable, as the impasse reached in Anglican–Methodist negotiations has made abundantly clear.

This chapter was drafted before the crucial votes were taken by the Convocations of Canterbury and York and by the Methodist Conference, and now, on the day following the adverse Anglican decision, I find myself revising what originally I had hopefully written. The achievement of union between an episcopal Church and one in which ministers had not hitherto been episcopally ordained might have provided the framework for a more comprehensive Church of England in the 1970s as well as providing a pattern for advance in other countries. But these hopes have been dashed to the ground, at least for the time being, and those who have laboured for so many years to forge a workable basis for union have now to pick up the pieces and start again.

First of all it is necessary to take stock of the situation and see what progress has been made and what has led to the present impasse. In spite of the strong and vocal minority of Methodists who opposed the scheme on the ground that their distinctively evangelical tradition was in danger of being compromised, the Conference at Birmingham decisively registered its vote to go forward with more than a 77 per cent majority. That surely means, as the Archbishop of Canterbury said in an interview immediately after the result was announced, that there can be no going back on the commitment to unity, especially when the large Anglican majority of 69 per cent in the combined votes of the upper and lower houses of both convocations is taken into account.

The judgement of the signatories to the final report on the conversations still stands:

> the move towards union has already begun: in many fields where our two Churches co-operate in pastoral endeavour, local plans formed since 1965 have been based on the assumption that union is coming within the foreseeable future. To go back on this at the present time would be a major disaster, not merely for the cause of unity, but for the Christian mission itself.[3]

Unhappily, the Anglican vote did not reach the required 75 per cent for implementing the first stage of the scheme. It was clear from the debate, which gathered momentum up to the very last moment, that a combination of strangely ill-assorted forces was likely to render the outcome problematic. In the end the alliance of a group of high churchmen and conservative evangelicals defeated the proposals, though their reasons for voting against them were strikingly contradictory.

On the one hand a large number of Anglo-Catholics, amongst whom the Bishop of Willesden was prominent, were sharply critical of the proposed Service of Reconciliation on the ground that it leaves the meaning of episcopal laying on of hands open to private interpretation.[4] In their view, this would be tantamount to repudiating Anglican formularies in which it is decreed that ordination to the threefold ministry of bishop, priest and deacon is to be by episcopal consecration. There must be no ambiguity. The *necessity* of episcopal ordination must be clearly recognized and stated. Otherwise the Church of England will be held to have abandoned the catholic tradition to which it is at present committed.

On the other hand a considerable body of clergy and laity were opposed to the scheme for precisely the opposite reason: the belief that the Service of Reconciliation suggested the possibility of the reordination of Methodist ministers and left the door open to a tacit acceptance of the doctrine of the historic episcopate. In their view the declared intention of the two Churches to unite on the basis of agreed doctrine and practice is sufficient without any formal reconciliation of ministries.

To these conflicting voices was added the intervention of Lord Fisher, the former Archbishop of Canterbury, who conducted a private campaign against the pledge to bring about union in two stages. Favouring, with certain qualifications, the principle behind stage one, Lord Fisher has been critical of the pledge to integrate the organizational structures in the second stage.[5] He claims that nobody knows what this would mean and he holds that the structure of a national Church would need to take into account the views of other Churches besides that of the Methodists. Moreover he views with alarm the possible jeopardizing of the Church of England's relationship with the State if there is any premature commitment to organic union. Lord Fisher would prefer to see the two Churches preserve their organizational independence for the foreseeable future, while co-operating together on the basis of mutual recognition.

It is difficult to assess how influential Lord Fisher's views have been. They have certainly appealed to many who do not want to see radical changes in ecclesiastical structures. But that is precisely what is required. While Christian unity, expressed in a mutual recognition of ministries and intercommunion is of crucial importance, it is not by any means enough if antiquated structures and creaking machinery have to be radically reformed. Lord Fisher appears to be reasonably content with the *status quo* or at least to believe that it cannot be rationalized. This is the point at which an increasing number of Christians of all denominations profoundly disagree with him.

Unfortunately the issue has been further bedevilled by charges that the scheme was being steam-rollered without full opportunity for all sides of the case to be presented at the deanery and parochial levels where opinion was tested; and many claimed that they were being stampeded by the Establishment. Thus political considerations and even sociological prejudices, such as a suspicion of Free Churchmen and their background, may have had an unduly important influence on the way in which some people cast their votes.

All of this added up to a confusion of dubious theology and politics, and the opportunity for advance was lost. We now have to ask what is the way ahead. There are some who believe that, given time, a sufficient majority will crystallize in the Anglican Church to approve the scheme in its original form. Certainly no other proposal appears to stand the slightest chance of winning agreement in the foreseeable future. But are the differences likely to be resolved at the level on which the discussions have been conducted? Have we at last got to face the fact that to begin with conciliar agreement is to start from the wrong end? Even if the decision of the Anglican Convocations had been favourable, its implementation at the grass roots would have been the crucial test, and it is clear that there would have been many dissidents and still more who would have done absolutely nothing through sheer apathy or inertia.

What is now needed is a ground swell: the development of areas of ecumenical experiment and commitment, involving not only Anglicans and Methodists but all those of any denomination who are prepared to participate; and out of this may emerge the structure of a new Church of England, which will be not the piecing together of fragments from the past but an organic growth of the Body of Christ. Those who want to know the shape of things to come or are sure that their own structural pattern is the necessary framework for unity will be alarmed at the uncertainty which now faces us. But uncertainty may well be the only road to opportunity and the fulfilment of God's purpose. It becomes clearer every day that the old denominational structures will have to crumble if the Church is to be free for the demands of the hour.

Does this mean that conversations between the existing denominations at the national level should be discontinued or discouraged and everything be left to local enterprise until a new pattern emerges? Not at all. The achievement of a mutual recognition of ministries and full intercommunion remains an indispensable framework for further advance. But it is now doubtful whether much progress can be made without the involvement of the other major denominations; apart from that any national agreement is unlikely to reflect the realities of the situation at the local level. In this connexion the culmination of Congregational–Presbyterian union may well assume much greater significance than it appeared to have before the breakdown of the Anglican–Methodist scheme. In short, it is vital to press forward towards the reunion of the major Churches in these islands, whatever the setbacks and frustrations, believing that in the end the Spirit, who has impelled us thus far to unity, will prevail.

There is one further aspect of the existing national structures which we need to take into account and which, if tackled, could materially contribute to the breakthrough we have been discussing. I refer to the proliferation of the missionary societies, each with its own headquarters and separate organization, of which mention was made in an earlier chapter. At the risk of some repetition I take up the point again to stress that a parochial outlook is one of the main reasons why so many Christians remain content with the *status quo* and find it so difficult to look beyond the horizons of their traditional concerns. If there is to be a real breakthrough out of the structures which at all levels impede the mission of the Church, a far broader vision is required, which will shake us out of our complacency and enable us to see the purpose of God in global terms. Without this we are likely to stay embedded in the comfortable seclusion of our parochial interests.

In spite of everything that has been written and said in recent years, the vast majority of Christians still regard the world-wide mission of the Church as the special concern of a few enthusiasts. On 'Missionary Sunday' the work of a particular society may be featured, and on other occasions consciences salved by contributions to Christian Aid, Oxfam, Save the Children Fund and the like. I do not want to minimize the generosity displayed, or the genuine concern to help which is evoked by these appeals. But I do not think it will be disputed that for the most part the response is spasmodic and that comparatively few Christians see themselves as really involved in a world-wide enterprise.

The integration of Church and Missionary Society would

be a first step towards changing the picture. The results would not become apparent overnight, but more and more people would come to see that when the Church is present anywhere, it is committed everywhere. Instead of special offerings being devoted to the work of a missionary society, the budget of the congregation would include a certain proportion earmarked for mission in every part of the world. This is already happening in some places, but imaginative leadership is being hampered by the dichotomy in thinking which is perpetuated by our outmoded structures. The introverted attitude has to be shattered at all levels and the windows opened to the inescapable connexion between mission and unity.

Finally we turn to the regional structures. Certain anomalies immediately cry out for attention and, given the resolve, could be tackled without delay. Paramount amongst these is the fact that, irrespective of denomination, regional organization is largely based on geography: a given territory has determined the boundaries rather than the incidence of population. This is the legacy of a past age when people tended to live in the same locality from the time they were born to the time they died. But all that has changed with the constant movement of population, the drift from the countryside to the city and the massive redistribution of workers and their families following industrial development. These and other factors, making for wholly new configurations of society, render the old ecclesiastical boundaries outdated. Some dioceses, for example, are much too large; others much too scattered. Again, some areas of population which have come to constitute an obvious demographical unit are not served by any corresponding ecclesiastical organization. This has led to a plea for rethinking boundaries in terms of the way in which people are actually related in modern society: in terms of human zones rather than of geographical areas.[6]

A second matter that requires attention is co-operation in the redrawing of boundaries. As things stand, the regional organization of different denominations is totally unco-ordinated, and this will raise increasing and unnecessary difficulties as local ecumenical experiments get under way. It also contributes to the problems of communication with government and voluntary bodies, which are so often frustrated in dealing with the complexity of the ecclesiastical network. With the publication of the Maud Report on regional and local government and the recent proposals for redrawing the boundaries of parliamentary constituencies, it is high time for the Churches to do something to set their own house in order, taking into account official measures that are likely to be implemented in the near future.

All this is mainly administrative. Much more important is the attitude taken by regional ecclesiastical authorities to experiments being made within their area of jurisdiction and the way in which they face their own responsibilities in the days ahead. Not every experiment is going to be successful and there is danger that some of the adventurers who are prepared to go out on a limb will become discouraged when they encounter unexpected difficulties. The spirit of adventure has to be kept alive and pioneer projects initiated in promising situations. Here the role of diocesan bishops and superintendent ministers is of cardinal importance. If they are over-cautious or unimaginative or too preoccupied with routine administration to give their minds to anything new, the strategy of which I have been speaking will suffer. Unfortunately most of these men are overburdened with the problems of keeping the ecclesiastical machinery working. We need greater devolution, smaller dioceses and more co-ordination between bishops and superintendent ministers of other Churches. Above all, those holding these positions of responsibility have to be convinced that stimulating ecumenical concern is a first priority: a conviction likely to be greatly reinforced in the light of the breakdown of the scheme for Anglican-Methodist union. On the whole, the kind of people who have been elected to these offices in recent years are inclined to be sympathetic, in some cases very sympathetic, to this approach.

But when that has been said, the positive influence that can be exerted by those in key positions does not go nearly far enough. Looking to the future, what is required is a regional centre for every main population zone to provide inspiration and leadership for the whole Church within its orbit. It should be a place where creative thinking is being done, where a programme of continuing education for clergy, ministers and lay people is organized, where experiments are made in worship, where music and the arts find imaginative expression, and where specialized service to the whole community is focused. In other words, a regional centre, manned by a carefully selected team, should provide a ministry to the whole area which no individual congregation or localized experiment could possibly offer.

Some would claim that this is the proper function of the Anglican cathedral and its staff, but it could hardly be maintained that the purpose outlined is being fulfilled, except in very limited respects. Up till quite recently the staff of a cathedral consisted in the main of those engaged in administrative duties within the diocese, and they were usually chosen with this in mind. Consequently the ministry of the cathedral itself was left largely in the hands of the dean and one canon, who normally acted as treasurer. It is hardly surprising that this should have meant that little more could be done than arrange for the regular offering of worship and such special services as occasion demanded. Anything like a centre of imaginative leadership for the whole diocese was virtually out of the question.

The position has somewhat changed following the report of a commission set up by the Church Assembly in 1958. Convinced of the significant part that cathedrals could play in the life of the nation, the members of the commission recommended certain important changes of policy.

> Our suggestion is that there should be in every Cathedral a Dean and two residentiary Canons holding no other benefice or demanding diocesan office but engaged solely in Cathedral work. We would include in the term 'Cathedral work' assistance to the Bishop in his cure of souls of the whole Diocese. For the Cathedral is the Bishop's Church and the Mother Church of the Diocese and its work should not be regarded as being confined to the Cathedral Close. This minimal constitution of a Dean and two Canons would enable the Cathedral to act as a collegiate body in which prayer was offered daily for the diocese, and to which the parishes were welcomed; and to be the centre from which aid of a pastoral or theological nature could be dispensed for diocesan needs. Canons might undertake such work as the direction of Ordination Candidates, and post-ordination training; or advise the Bishop and clergy on pastoral or sociological or industrial questions. We are quite clear that these two

> Canons ought not to be Suffragan Bishops, Assistant Bishops, or Archdeacons, or to be appointed to such substantial diocesan administrative work as Director of Education or Secretary of the Diocesan Board of Finance. We believe that in nearly every diocese two such Canons could be fully and usefully employed without waste of manpower.[7]

As a result of this recommendation, legislation was passed in 1964 to the effect that every cathedral must have a dean and two canons exclusively concerned with its ministry and not employed in administrative duties for the diocese; their salaries were to be found by the Church Commissioners. This has at least opened the doors to new possibilities, but it must be confessed that there is a long road ahead if any radical changes are to be made in this traditionally most conservative of British institutions. The image of Barchester still prevails and, although the attempt is being made here and there to break free from the ancient pattern, the average cathedral and its chapter have all the appearance of a medieval anachronism, unrelated to the world of the twentieth century.[8]

The Free Churches have scarcely begun to come to terms with the requirements to which I have referred. The large city church conceives of its role as a major preaching centre after the Victorian model, drawing its congregation from a wide area and often denuding congregations in the outlying districts. So far from serving the churches of the area, it is more like a parasite, drawing away the life blood from the region round about. Where such churches are strong in membership, they are of growingly doubtful relevance. Where they are weak—and this is more often the case—

they are exposed as white elephants, with large and mostly antiquated premises which are a burden to maintain.

Are there any signs of a new pattern emerging? In many ways the most promising experiments are being made in Coventry, with its new cathedral, its chapel of unity, its association with strong Free Churches, its hospitable attitude to the Roman Catholic Church, and its varied staff. Interesting things are, of course, happening elsewhere, as at Southwark, Bristol and Liverpool, while St Paul's Cathedral and Westminster Abbey are *sui generis* in the sense that they are national shrines, having a unique role to play in the country at large. But Coventry is at the centre of a fairly typical diocese, and the rebuilding of an imaginative modern cathedral alongside the ruins of the old one, destroyed by Nazi bombing, has afforded the opportunity of taking a fresh look at the function such a cathedral can fulfil.

The devastating air attacks on the heart of the city introduced a new word into the English language: to be 'coventrated' was the castration of an urban area involving the total destruction of the old with the promise of building something entirely new. In the public imagination at home and abroad all this was focused on the cathedral and Sir Basil Spence's design attracted the attention of people from every part of the world. Hundreds of thousands of visitors make their way there every year, and the image of the Church and its ministry is being profoundly affected by what they see. Here at least is a cathedral which gives the impression of being the very heart of a modern city.

The provost and the staff he has gathered round him are fully alert to the need for making the cathedral relevant to the whole life of the community. 'A passion of mine has always been', writes H. C. N. Williams:

> . . . that the Church makes sense only if the Church is the expression of the wholeness in the community. The Church is irrelevant to the community if it doesn't give the impression of being a coherent society within an incoherent community. The Church has not only got to be the pattern of the unity of society but it has also got to be the means of expressing that unity when it is discovered. This involves the Church mixing itself up with the community a great deal more than it does, involving itself in the tensions and cross-currents of society, understanding them, and meeting society on the vast area of common ground that exists between them.[9]

This is the vision of a cathedral that has inspired the provost and his colleagues, and they have not been slow to experiment with many and varied forms of ministry. Traditional Anglican worship has been adapted to make it as meaningful as possible to the large congregations that often gather there. Music and drama find a natural home within its precincts, and the staff itself consists of those engaged in specialized ministries in civic affairs, industry, schools, colleges, voluntary organizations and the like. It could, of course, be claimed that such ministries are not, strictly speaking, dependent on the cathedral, and could be exercised by a central team serving the city and diocesan area. Nevertheless, they are the cathedral staff, and the cathedral is the centre of their worship and life. This alone gives a focus to their ministry, without which it would lack coherence.

As far as I have been able to ascertain, the major omission at Coventry in the functions I have depicted as ideally desirable in a modern cathedral is the surprising absence of any comprehensive programme of continuing education for clergy and laity in the diocese. The cathedral library has the nucleus of a good modern collection but it is not widely used, while the bookshop's large trade is mainly in paperbacks which one might reasonably expect to find on a parish bookstall. It seems to me that one of the first responsibilities of a cathedral church is to attend to the crying need for a new approach to Christian education, and to recruit a team set free for corporate thinking and research, as well as for lectures and seminars designed to expound the Faith and relate it to the whole life of a modern conurbation.[10] All the same, in many respects Coventry points the way forward to what a cathedral should be: the beginning of a regional breakthrough to be further exploited.

However, the picture is not so encouraging when one asks what is the relationship between the cathedral and the parishes of the diocese. The answer has to be equivocal. Some look to it as a centre of inspiration, particularly welcoming the new image it has given to the Church as a living institution. Others regard the cathedral with suspicion and even with some hostility, believing that it draws away into a central congregation those who should be identified with their own parish churches. In part this is the reflection of out-of-date parochial attitudes, but it also represents a tension in regard to the function of a cathedral within the diocese. Has the role of the servant been sufficiently established in both thought and practice over against the image of the octopus drawing everything within its tentacles?

What of the Free Churches? It has to be confessed that the chapel of unity has so far been little more than a symbol; and even the recent appointment of its Warden, the Congregationalist Geoffrey Beck, to the cathedral staff and the allocation to him of a non-Chapter seat in the chancel are a declaration of intent rather than substantial progress towards the creation of an ecumenical team ministry for the city and region. Furthermore, the development of an effective Christian service centre has proceeded very slowly.

Part of the difficulty lies in the strength of the different Free Churches in the centre of the city. The Methodist Central Hall, Warwick Road Congregational Church and Queens Road Baptist Church are all amongst the most influential Free Churches in the country, served by a succession of notable ministers and each attracting large congregations, while the thriving St Columba's Presbyterian Church is not far away. This is an unusual situation, to put it mildly. Happily there is good co-operation between the ministers and cathedral staff and a flourishing Council of Churches in which they all participate. But this falls far short of the regional team ministry of which I have been speaking. The Free Churches have not been encouraged by others in their denominations to see their role in these terms at all; discussions with the cathedral staff have not yet produced specific joint plans, and the type of minister to which they have been accustomed tends to be an individualist who would not naturally think of himself as a specialist within a group. Before much progress can be made towards developing the kind of regional team ministry which I have been adumbrating, a new generation may have to be trained to think of their vocation in an altogether different way. That will be the theme of the next chapter. In the meantime we may be thankful for the imaginative pioneering that has been so markedly evidenced at Coventry and see in it a pointer to the road ahead in many other regions.

All of this is but a beginning. The way ahead is bound to be long and arduous, and will be marked by many pitfalls and roadblocks. Nor do we easily break free from our shackles. Nevertheless, the breakthroughs will occur, regionally as well as nationally, when it is clearly recognized that the Church is deformed by its struggle to survive, but reformed when it is really committed to ministry and mission.[11]

Chapter Five

Towards the Renewal of Ministry

The renewal of the Church and the reformation of its structures inevitably raise questions about the ministry. What is its true nature? Of whom should it consist? How should those recruited conceive their role? What training do they require? Nobody can doubt that there is widespread dissatisfaction with many of the answers that have been given to these questions in the past; and we now face confusion, amounting almost to a *malaise*, spreading more and more to clergy and laity alike. The number of candidates for ordination has been falling sharply; there is restiveness amongst theological students as they contemplate their future and the training they are receiving; men of all denominations are forsaking the professional ministry for vocations which seem to them to be more significant; others, and some of the ablest among them, leave the parish or pastoral ministry for more specialized service; while those who remain are often burdened by doubts as to whether they have made a mistake and whether their role is a defensible one in the world in which we are living.

There are many factors contributing to this widespread *malaise*, as I have called it: doubts about the truth and relevance of Christian beliefs as traditionally understood, uncertainty about the role of the Church in the modern world, economic hardship and personal loneliness, to mention only the most obvious. In varying measure I have dealt with these problems elsewhere in this book. Here I want to begin by raising another issue which I believe to be at the centre of the confusion now prevailing: the rediscovery of the role of the laity in the Christian mission.

In the past to 'enter the Church' was the equivalent of becoming ordained; and for many people the Church still means the hierarchy and the clergy with laymen as hangers-on. All this is rapidly changing, not least in the Roman Church, which has hitherto been exclusively clerically dominated. At the Second Vatican Council the concept of the people of God began to be taken seriously, though the implications of doing so have hardly as yet been realized. As for the rest, there is no escaping the central role of the laity in the call to mission. 'Any embodiment of the Church in contemporary society will be an apostolate of the laity in the world. This is the crucial fact about renewal of the Church in an organizational world.'[1]

In a sense there is nothing new about all of this. The Churches that stand in the tradition of the Reformation have always insisted, in theory at least, that the people of God are in the apostolic succession, and they have appealed to the Scriptures in support of this contention. While ancient Israel was dependent on charismatic leadership, it was the nation as a whole that was called to be the instrument of the divine purpose; and the Church was the new Israel, 'a chosen race, a royal priesthood, a holy nation, God's own people'.[2] In this sense Luther spoke of the 'priesthood of all believers'. He did not mean what the phrase has subsequently been taken to imply: the competence of the individual soul before God, the right of access to God without a human intermediary. While that is a derivative idea of great importance, Luther was concerned to assert that *the whole Church* had succeeded to the priesthood, not simply a select group within it.

The rediscovery of this doctrine, not as a theoretical tenet but as the very essence of the Church's mission, has thrown a large question mark over the professional ministry and that is why many have begun to wonder whether their vocation might not find more effective fulfilment in secular occupations. The traditional image is being turned upside down. Instead of the Church being pictured as the hierarchy and the clergy with laymen as hangers-on, precisely the opposite is beginning to be suggested. For example, Gibson Winter writes, 'The ministry is usually conceived today as the work of clergymen with auxiliary aids among the laity; ministry in the servant Church is the work of laity in the world with auxiliary help from theological specialists.'[3] In the face of comments like these it is scarcely surprising that the man responsible for a parish or congregation begins to ask whether he has missed his vocation.

Gibson Winter's remark does, of course, betray its Protestant origin. Those in the Catholic tradition would be quick to point out that it ignores the sacramental character of the priesthood and that this specialized ministry is essential to the life of the Church, even though an increasing number of Catholic theologians would argue that it is the people of God that celebrates, with the priest as the ordained agent and representative. Nevertheless they hold that, whatever the role of the laity and however much the past imbalance needs to be redressed, only the ordained priest may celebrate the sacrament of Holy Communion and exercise the authority which has been vested in him by episcopal action; without this ministry the Church would be sapped of its life blood.

But most Christians within the Reformed Churches would be unlikely to accept Gibson Winter's aphorism just as it stands. While Luther enunciated the doctrine of the priesthood of all believers, he did not mean to imply thereby that priests in the narrower sense were expendable. For the sake of order, he held, some have to be set aside to serve in the name of the whole congregation and to perform certain stated functions, though they do so only in a representative capacity. They belong to no order that can be set above the Church; they are priests because the Church exercises its priesthood through them.[4] Nevertheless their function is distinctive. The majority of those within the main stream of Protestantism would follow Luther in this, insisting on the separation of an order of men to the ministry of the Word and sacraments; and even those less rigid in their restriction of these functions tend in practice to reserve them for those who have been specifically ordained. Thus Gibson Winter's reference to 'theological specialists', perhaps unintentionally, conveys all too narrow an impression to do duty as a model for the servant Church in the world. There is a continuing and central place for the ministry of the Word and sacraments as well as for other types of specialized leadership in a Church where the apostolate of the laity is accorded the fullest prominence.

All this is undoubtedly true. Nevertheless the fact remains that the average parson is disturbed about his role in the modern world. In an age of specialization he feels he is expected to be the jack of all trades and master of none: preacher, celebrant, liturgist, administrator, counsellor, spiritual adviser, teacher, social worker, youth leader, community centre worker, industrial and hospital chaplain and civic odd job man, all rolled into one. As Canon Taylor points out in his trenchant paper on the subject,[5] this is the hang-over of 'the ideal of the Renaissance Man, informed and at home in every art and every science',[6] the omnicompetent clergyman, an anachronism in the twentieth century. If the medical profession were to be so conceived, 'it would mean that as soon as a medical student had passed his second degree of Bachelor of Medicine he would take his place in some local general practice, combining the work of a physician with surgery, dentistry, obstetrics, preventive medicine and responsibility for public health; only those who were appointed to the big teaching hospitals would continue with any specialization, let alone do any research. Medically that would put the clock back just about a century.'[7]

This is an issue that must be faced. So far we have failed to do so because we have become accustomed to distinguishing between ministers on a hierarchical rather than on a functional basis: as archbishops, bishops, deans, moderators, presidents, superintendents, incumbents, pastors, deacons and assistant ministers.[8] In the New Testament the classification of the ministry was according to the gifts of the Spirit: 'Some should be apostles, some prophets, some evangelists, some pastors and teachers'.[9] Translated into terms of the modern situation, this can be interpreted with Canon Taylor as follows: 'God has given some to be overseers and team leaders, some to interpret the Gospel in terms of community and social ethics, some to enter into dialogue with other faiths and work out a new apologetic for a secular world, some to do counselling and casework, and some to be theologians.'[10] No one man can do everything; ministry in the narrower as well as the broader sense must be diversified. In passing, we may note that the acceptance of this conclusion would raise serious questions about the basis on which candidates for the ministry are at present selected.

The need for specialization inevitably points to the development of team ministries which for the future will have to be regarded as the norm rather than the exception. As yet we have done little more than make a few tentative experiments, but, as in so many other matters demanding the Church's attention, time is not on our side. Quite apart from the obvious requirements of a more specialized ministry, there are other considerations which point in the same direction. One of the most insidious problems that the parson faces today is that of loneliness.[11] Whether he be the incumbent of a large city parish, a missioner on a new housing estate or the minister of a small congregation, he is all the time concerned with breaking down the barriers of isolation between people and building community from a base of loneliness within himself. The encouragement of bishops and superintendents and the sympathy of his colleagues expressed in meetings of fraternals are no substitute for working together with others in co-operative service. Perhaps this is a much larger factor in accounting for the drift from the professional ministry than anybody has yet realized. What is certain is that in many cases loneliness leads to introversion and a self-regarding defensiveness in human relations. How far is this the explanation of the fact that so many people find the parson unapproachable? At all events, signs are not lacking that the young are more and more looking to the attractiveness of team ministries, and the possibility of engaging in them may well be an important factor in recruitment in the days to come.

Overarching these considerations is the economic factor:

the decline in the number of candidates for ordination and the impossibility of providing adequate stipends for a proliferation of isolated ministries. The Free Churches are already facing this as a matter of urgency and, while the Anglican and Roman Churches are cushioned to some extent by much larger resources, the day of reckoning for them cannot be postponed indefinitely, particularly in the light of the rapid rise in the cost of living. The idea of one priest to one parish, one minister to one congregation has to go. We simply cannot afford all the duplication of effort and dissipation of resources that it entails.

The rationalization that would become practicable by the development of team ministries becomes plain when we begin to see how responsibilities could be divided and shared. As long as the concept of the omnicompetent parson prevails, the multiplication of professional clergymen is the inevitable consequence. The abandonment of this as an ideal opens the way to the use of ordained men earning their living in secular occupations and the more effective deployment of laymen. The conduct of worship and the administration of the sacraments need not be the exclusive prerogative of those who are the paid full-time servants of the Church. Men and (dare I say?) women could be ordained to the ministry of the Word and sacraments, as members of a team, without that carrying with it any implication of their being full-time professionals. On the other hand, the Church would need salaried specialists for organization, counselling, spiritual direction (for which there are too few qualified people), group leadership, teaching and ministry to different aspects of the community: civic, industrial and institutional. A much more flexible pattern than at present obtains needs to be evolved; and this would probably mean the recruitment of a smaller number of professionals, of a higher standard, better qualified, and more adequately remunerated.

This raises the whole question of ministerial training, a subject now under urgent review in all the Churches. If I have been right in arguing that specialization in team ministries is bound to be the increasing demand in the years to come, a much more radical reappraisal is necessary than is envisaged in minor alterations to the curriculum. Some of the basic assumptions that have hitherto been taken for granted will need to be critically examined, and this will entail changes that will seem nothing short of revolutionary.

The sense of deep disquiet felt by many theological students of all denominations about the training that they are at present receiving was forcibly expressed in a manifesto produced at the end of a conference recently held under the auspices of the Student Christian Movement. Representing thirty-eight different colleges, they declared that the education they were receiving in no way equipped them for the task to which they believed themselves called, and they made the following twelve demands for urgent consideration and immediate action:

1. We should live among those whom we are being educated to serve.
2. Our education should be fully ecumenical.
3. Our education should be associated with the continuing education of ministers and lay training, and should take place in study, action and seminar teams.
4. Our education should take advantage of existing institutions of higher training.
5. Besides a permanent staff, there should be access to persons with specialist knowledge.

6. Theology should be built up in the study of cultures and society.
7. Our education should be in integrated practical courses.
8. Our education must be geared towards specialist ministries.
9. We must be made aware of new techniques.
10. We must develop forms of worship that are worthy of the people of God.
11. Our education must be under constant evaluation and revision.
12. Authority and responsibility must be in the hands of both students and staff.

This is a formidable catalogue of requirements, and it would be rash in the extreme to write it off as typical of student rebellion, especially at a time when the underlying causes of the revolt of the young have to be taken with the utmost seriousness. In some respects, indeed, the manifesto does not go far enough. It would be possible to implement many of these proposals without facing the most radical questions that need to be asked about the whole approach to ministerial training which we have inherited from the past. Tinkering is not enough. Only by a complete overhaul of principles and practice will we begin to see what is really required.

The fundamental question that has to be raised is whether an academic theological education is an adequate preparation for the Christian ministry today. Hitherto it has generally been taken for granted that a university degree in theology is the ideal qualification for a candidate for ordination to possess. Oxford has virtually set the standard, even for those who are most critical of what they believe to be its far too antiquarian curriculum. It has gone without saying that four main subjects are the basic ingredients of any reputable course: Old Testament, New Testament, Christian Doctrine and Church History. Other subjects, such as the philosophy of religion, the comparative study of religion and the psychology and sociology of religion, have been added as optional extras, or in more radical reformulations of the curriculum have been married to the traditional subjects. But, whatever the variations and permutations, the ideal has remained an academic discipline; and where candidates for ordination have not been qualified for admission to university courses, the theological colleges which have undertaken their training have largely modelled their curricula on the same basis. The assumption has been that if a student is not capable of working for a university degree, he should be given as rigorous an academic course as he can follow; for him a second best is the only option. But there is no doubt what the best is.

Behind this approach to ministerial training is the conviction that the most important qualification is a trained mind. Given the background of an exacting intellectual discipline, a man will be able to tackle practical affairs with an assured touch. Particularly is this the case, it has been argued, with the Christian ministry which is charged with preaching and teaching the Faith in an age when more and more people are receiving higher education. This has been a major line of defence for retaining the Oxford School of Theology in its traditional form and regarding it as a bastion of academic excellence and an ideal for ministerial training.

Now I do not believe that such an argument should be dismissed out of hand as sheer conservatism. There is much to be said for the view that rigorous intellectual discipline, involving detailed and accurate study of ancient texts, does educate the trained mind which is so sorely needed in a world ruled by irrational passion. But in an age when professional specialization has come to be taken for granted, the thesis that a man who has studied 'Greats' at Oxford and has steeped himself in the thought, the history and the literature of the classical period is fully qualified for the civil and diplomatic service is problematical to say the least. And when it comes to the Christian ministry, it is by no means self-evident that a first-class degree in theology will equip a man to expound the Faith in a way that will make sense in contemporary society, even if it were admitted that this is all that he is called to do. But how far does the image of the scholar-parson or the Victorian preacher underlie the argument anyway?

It makes no difference to what I have been saying to object that Oxford is a bad example to take, that Cambridge is more open to the winds of change, that the Scottish universities give greater attention to modern theology, that Bristol and Hull have devised courses in conjunction with the departments of philosophy and sociology.[12] Nor is it any more to the point to cast envious eyes across the Atlantic where an increasing variety of practical subjects have been crammed into the curriculum and turned the passion for degree chasing into a veritable rat race. The merits and demerits of different courses will continue to be debated, and doubtless there is always room for improvement. But my contention is that, however good they are, however integrated into the whole field of academic enquiry, they are not in themselves, nor can they be made to be, an adequate preparation for the ministry of the Church in the modern world. Let there be no misunderstanding. I am not opposed to university courses in theology. Quite the contrary. I am all in favour of as many students as possible pursuing the most rigorous academic study, and I believe this to be a first-rate *preparation* for ministerial training. Moreover, it is a serious matter that a diminishing number of candidates for ordination are not up to the standard required. But this is not training for the varied ministry needed in the days ahead. That is the proper job of the theological colleges.

Here precisely is the rub. When we look at the theological colleges, we find that most of them are modelled on university departments, with the same core curriculum and varying flexibility in regard to practically oriented subjects. Where these colleges are closely related to universities, suitably qualified students concentrate on working for degrees; the rest pursue the same kind of course within the college at a level adapted to their own powers, playing at being academics. Hence the tensions that arise when those with little or no linguistic aptitude are made to acquire a smattering of Hebrew and Greek. The assumption appears to be that any educated minister should be able to read the Scriptures in the original languages; and where a man is unable to reach any degree of mastery, he should at least know what he has failed to do and be able to use a dictionary. In the case of those colleges which are isolated from university cities, the tendency to take university courses as a model may be less marked, but their influence in large measure still prevails. What is needed is a radical rethinking of ministerial training in its own terms and in relation to the Church of the future, freed from the academic presuppositions of the past. This will entail a programme which is tailored for the man or woman who has no university degree in theology and at the same time is sufficiently challenging for those who have such a background. That may require different kinds of colleges preparing students for different kinds of ministry, a number of colleges being justified not, as at present, on geographical or denominational grounds, but on the variety of courses available. In this connexion the plea that theological colleges should be open to laymen and become centres of lay training may be very much to the point; for, if team ministries are to be the pattern of the future and lay leaders are to take their place alongside those professionally qualified, there is everything to be said for their training being undertaken together.

The objection will undoubtedly be raised that no Church regards an academic degree in theology as the *sole* qualification for the Christian ministry, nor does it conceive of any of its theological colleges as having a purely academic task either for those with a university training behind them or for those entering directly from school, professional or business life. The General Ordination Examination of the Church of England, for example, is devised with a different purpose in view, and the curriculum is planned accordingly. That is true. But the main point I am making still stands. Courses in theological colleges, whatever their additions and adaptations, are still in the main basically influenced and shaped by the traditional conviction that the core of any curriculum must be the Old and New Testaments, Church History and Christian Doctrine. The question I am asking is whether a radical reappraisal does not start elsewhere: with the relationship of the Faith and the Church to the modern world, and not with a historical study. To put it crudely, this means starting with the world and going backwards, instead of starting with the Bible and hoping you will find a point of connexion with the contemporary scene. It means the involvement of the theological college in the society of which it is a part, with students living, not in closed communities, but amongst those whom they will ultimately serve, studying the Bible and doing theology out of a living situation. Other subjects, such as sociology, liturgy and pastoralia, will not then be additions to the curriculum, but will inevitably arise out of the setting.

We may go further. Universities are now being subjected to radical questioning about their educational methods: about the usefulness of lectures, the desirability of a rigid set of course requirements, the examination system and the criteria for assessment. Clearly changes are on the way, many of them bewildering and unpalatable to those steeped in traditional assumptions. But the difficulty reformers have to face is that a degree-granting institution has to maintain recognized academic standards and objective criteria for assessing a student's performance. It is, therefore, hard to see how universities can meet the most radical demands that are being made upon them. If, however, ministerial training were to be set free from enslavement to diplomas and degrees, it would be much more open to the process of learning, starting from where students actually are and from the questions they are really asking. Educationalists are increasingly stressing that learning springs from motivation, and a prepackaged course is no stimulus to the enquiring mind. Learning should be exciting exploration, but this is so often stultified by the didactic method of instruction and the looming requirements of examinations, performance in which is to no small degree a matter of technique. Training for the ministry demands the development of initiative and responsibility, which is much more likely to flower in a free context where the onus is on the student and the members of the staff are regarded as resource personnel.

This does not mean a relaxing of standards or an undisciplined approach. On the contrary, it will be found to be far more exacting for staff and students alike. To object that, human nature being what it is, students will not respond except to the whip of requirements, assignments and examinations betrays a peculiar expectation of a pitifully low standard of entry. If this is the correct estimate of any candidate for the ministry, then he should be automatically disqualified; for his life will have to be spent in self-discipline, and he had better learn that during his training. Perhaps many of the failures of the Christian ministry are to be traced back to a mistaken approach to earlier training. At any rate, we do well to consider whether the abandonment of diplomas and degrees by examination as the goal may not open the door to a much more creative and imaginative method of education. To contemplate such a proposal would be nothing short of revolutionary for many of those who have been accustomed to take the traditional system for granted. But are we irrevocably tied to it?

The arguments that university departments of theology and theological colleges sponsored by the Churches have totally different functions is likely to meet with resistance not only from those who are unprepared to face radical changes in the colleges concerned but also from some in the academic world, who regard universities as responsible for professional training. I have heard it argued that the university has a threefold responsibility: for pure research, for the pursuit of learning at the student level, and for professional training. This is a debatable question which raises the issue of the relationship between academic education and technological training. Some would maintain that universities are in danger of being diverted from their proper function by being turned into technological schools, and that this is bound up with the problems consequent upon the rapid expansion of higher education that is now taking place.

Whatever the outcome of this debate, I should want to claim that a department of theology is a special case. If it is too closely identified with training for the Christian ministry it will be suspect academically and will not attract students who are interested in pursuing the subject for its own sake. When I was engaged in negotiating the introduction of a doctoral programme in religion in the Faculty of Arts and Science at McMaster University in Canada, I was confronted with the deep-seated suspicion on the part of two successive deans of graduate studies, both Christian laymen, that theology was concerned with propaganda and was not a proper discipline for a candidate for a Ph.D. degree. They had to be persuaded that research would be fully open-ended and not tied in any way to ecclesiastical requirements. Moreover, the clear separation of a department of religion (so called because of the suspicion attaching to the word 'theology') from any connexion with ministerial training opened the door to a wide cross-section of some of the ablest students in the university enrolling in courses at all levels. During the negotiations at McMaster, the Dean of Arts and Science remarked: 'You have the opportunity of building the most completely open academic department in the university.'

From every point of view the importance of this can hardly be overrated. In Britain, at a time when the number of candidates for ordination has been sharply declining, new departments of theology have come into being and in some cases are over-subscribed through the influx of non-ministerial students. The most radical curriculum of all, devised by Professor Ninian Smart at Lancaster, points clearly to the road ahead. The modern secular university will not accept the presuppositions of Christian theology, but will increasingly insist on an open enquiry into the history, literature, philosophy and phenomena of religion. Exposure to such a course of study will come to be regarded more and more as a first-class liberal education, and incidentally an invaluable propaedeutic to preparation for the Christian ministry. But it will force the Churches to rethink what ministerial training as such involves.

If I am right in contending that the abandonment of academic criteria for ministerial training is the basic issue and that this entails the recasting of the role of theological colleges, the next question that will have to be faced is their denominational character in an ecumenical age. One of the major student demands referred to above was the insistence upon training being fully ecumenical. At the consultation on theological education recently held under the auspices of the World Council of Churches, astonishment was expressed by those coming from Africa and particularly from Asia that there was no ecumenical institution in Britain. They took it for granted that ministerial training had to be undertaken on an inter-denominational basis in the modern world. And the trend has been in the same direction elsewhere. Mention has only to be made of Union Theological Seminary in New York as an outstanding example of ecumenical co-operation.

In this country we have been far behind the times. It just does not make sense to insist on the desirability of a student for the ministry being trained in a college of his own denomination; and yet that is still the recognized and uncriticized policy. It is no reply to say that denominational theological colleges are often grouped together and share the same lectures and classes. This is only a small part of ministerial training. Much more important is the life of the community, learning to live together, to share in the common tasks and to understand different points of view. If the ministry of the future is going to involve ecumenical cooperation, then it is essential that those who will be participating in it should be trained together under the same roof. The grouping of colleges and the sharing of facilities is a step in the right direction, but it is only a very first step.

The experience of the British Council of Churches in its attempt to establish such a college has been scarcely encouraging. Following the Nottingham Conference in 1964, a committee was set up to explore possibilities, but it soon found that it was up against entrenched interests and the unwillingness of denominational colleges to jeopardize their own sectional interests. There have, of course, been notable exceptions which have gone some way towards remedying the situation. Mansfield College in Oxford has long opened its door to non-Congregationalists. In particular it has developed a fruitful relationship with Lutherans and has recently been engaged in negotiations with Wycliffe Hall, an Anglican institution, with a view to a merger. Mention should also be made of the uniting Westminster and Cheshunt Colleges, Cambridge. But these developments, important as they are, still fall short of anything that could be called a fully ecumenical venture.

At long last, however, there is prospect of a real breakthrough, due to the initiative of Dr J. S. Habgood, Principal of the Queen's College in Birmingham. Appointed in the autumn of 1967 to this famous Anglican institution, he found himself with splendid premises on a spacious campus close to the university, but with only a handful of students. Believing that the future lay with ecumenical theological education, he at once persuaded his governing council to elect a small committee to investigate the possibilities, and within a few months complete agreement was reached on a scheme which was unanimously adopted by the Council. It envisages a college open to students of all denominations, served by an ecumenical staff and with governing bodies representative of all the Churches. In view of the probable imminent closure of Handsworth Methodist College, the composition of the student community in the early stages will inevitably be mainly Anglican–Methodist, and the capital investment will be contributed entirely by these two churches. But from the very beginning students of other denominations will be welcome, and in the course of time it is hoped that Baptists, Congregationalists, Presbyterians and Roman Catholics will take an increasing share in the life of the college. Apart from the Bible Colleges, which have a more restricted theological basis, this is the first venture of its kind in the British Isles; and it will be interesting to see what the response will be. If the trend in the future is to be towards increasing ecumenical co-operation, then the days of the denominational theological college are numbered. Indeed, it may not be going too far to say that it is already something of an anachronism.

This poses an enormous practical problem. What is to be done with the multiplicity of theological colleges scattered all over the country? Most, if not all of them, are unviable units by modern standards from both the economic and educational points of view. The issue would still be an acute one if they were all full, but many of them are half empty, and sheer economic pressure is making some sort of rationalization inescapable.

Unfortunately the policy being pursued is one of amalgamation, bringing two colleges of the same denomination together in one set of premises; and even this is causing deep heart-searching. But quite apart from the fact that, with the exception of the colleges mentioned, this is not being done ecumenically and the old system is simply being shored up, the size of these amalgamated colleges is quite inadequate for the task they are going to be called upon to perform in the future. If, as Canon Taylor suggests,[13] the paramount need is to provide a variety of options for specialized ministry in group and team situations, then a much larger staff and a much larger student body is required than any existing theological college of any denomination has envisaged.

The problem has been faced in Canada by Professor Charles Fielding of Trinity College, Toronto. He, more than almost anyone else on the North American continent, has devoted himself to the study of theological education in the western world, and his conclusions deserve the widest and most careful attention. In an article published following a nation-wide survey, he argued that the range of subjects that now have to be handled demands a large and varied staff if superficiality is to be avoided. He therefore made the radical proposal that there should be no more than five theological centres in Canada with a minimum average of fifteen professors and one hundred and fifty students in each.[14] This would, of course, entail the closure of most of the existing theological colleges in Canada. The new world is generally more ready for change than the old; but entrenched interests are everywhere, and it will be no easy task to secure a measure of rationalization in Canada, even with Dr Fielding's great prestige behind it. In this country it will be immensely harder, but the problems have to be faced. Somehow a beginning must be made in forging a new pattern of ministerial training which matches the challenge with which the Church is now confronted.

Is there any way forward? Perhaps it may be helpful if I conclude this chapter by sketching an experiment that is now being made by my colleagues in the Selly Oak Colleges. I do so with some hesitation because I am involved in it myself, but it may serve as an illustration of what can be attempted if sufficient resources are brought together in one place and there is freedom to try out a fresh approach unhampered by rigid requirements. The experiment is still in its very early and tentative stages, but it is an attempt on an international and ecumenical basis to provide a course of training in Christian mission to six continents which may have something to say about the kind of preparation that those in the service of the Church are going to need for the days ahead.

The Selly Oak Colleges are a federation of nine, soon to be ten or eleven, residential institutions, each with its own governing body, principal and staff, and each having its own special ethos. They are situated four miles from the centre of the city of Birmingham, on the outskirts of Bournville Village on a campus donated by members of the Cadbury family. Each college stands in its own grounds and has its own corporate life, but there are also central playing-fields and buildings and a central staff of professors and lecturers who provide combined courses which relatively small institutions could not expect to offer. Hence the structure is very like Oxbridge, with its relationship of colleges to university.

Two major concerns have led to the foundation of the different institutions that make up the federation. The first of these is the world-wide mission of the Church. Starting with the establishment of Woodbrooke in 1903 as a centre for Quaker studies concentrating on international affairs and the service of Friends all over the world, other colleges were subsequently founded by different missionary societies: Kingsmead by the Methodists, the College of the Ascension by the Society for the Propagation of the Gospel (later the USPG), St Andrew's Hall by the Baptist Missionary Society, the Congregational Council for World Mission and the Presbyterian Overseas Missions Committees, Overdale by the Churches of Christ, and Crowther Hall, a new college built by the Church Missionary Society. To these colleges have come not only candidates for overseas service under the auspices of the British missionary societies, but students from North America, from most of the European countries, and from the third world. Roman Catholics, Orthodox and Lutherans have taken their place alongside Anglicans and Free Churchmen of all denominations. Every main Christian tradition and on an average about fifty countries are represented on the campus in any one year.

The second major concern has been the preparation of students for a wide variety of service to the community in this country and beyond. Westhill is a fully fledged college of education, specializing in religious instruction; but it is also the main centre for training youth leaders and wardens of community centres, and it has a special section for church education, principally for overseas students, who in many cases are preparing to be directors of training institutions in their own lands. Fircroft is a college of adult education, offering one-year courses in liberal studies to men from industry who have shown potentiality for leadership and an aptitude for further study; amongst their student body are to be found many typical rebels of the modern world. Avoncroft is a short-term college of further education, and plans are now being made for the building of Prospect Hall, the first college of adult education for the physically handicapped. Amongst the students enrolled in all the colleges are those preparing for various kinds of social work and recently the Ministry of Overseas Development has sponsored a course for selected social workers from the underdeveloped countries.

It has been necessary to give this brief description of Selly Oak because it explains the setting which has made possible the development of a new programme of training in Christian mission. Several years ago, the missionary societies responsible for some of the colleges had reached the stage where they were profoundly dissatisfied with traditional training for overseas service. They were resolved that such training must make maximum usage of all the resources available, that it must be realistically oriented to the kind of world in which we are living, and that it must be fully ecumenical. The result of long discussion led to the appointment of a Dean of Missionary Training in January 1968 who was charged with the responsibility of working out an entirely new course in collaboration with the central staff and the staffs of the various colleges. The Revd David Lyon, a member of the Iona Community, was seconded by the Church of Scotland and the United Church of Northern India for this purpose and he faced his task with the conviction that mission is indivisible and is the Church's calling everywhere in the world. The slogan 'Mission to six continents' had to be taken with the utmost seriousness.

Consequently a 'Training in Mission Semester' was devised to last six months, open to students whether they were preparing to go overseas and serve the Church in another land and another culture or whether they were going to remain in their own countries, in urban situations and the like, engaged in the Christian mission at home. The semester has been planned in fortnightly periods centring on Bible study in groups. A passage of Scripture has been selected for each fortnight; this is studied in four stages. In the first session the groups meet around the open Bible and examine the text as it stands; the second stage is concerned with detailed private study in the colleges making use of commentaries and critical apparatus; the third session is again in groups, sharing the results of digging in depth; and finally the passage is examined with a view to asking what it has to say to the world in which we are living. In the planning stages the fear was expressed that too much time was being given to one passage of Scripture. In the event students have complained that they have not had enough!

Around this core of Bible study, lectures and seminars and tutorials are arranged on a variety of related subjects. They are as follows: (1) The Church Universal, its traditions and tasks, its dialogue with the world, its ways of worship and styles of living; (2) The Mission of the Church, its theology and practice, including the principles of communication; (3) Experiments in Mission, in which men and women who are themselves engaged in situations of special significance speak and are questioned about their own experience; (4) Sociology and Social Work, the study of the structures of society, practical engagement through placements in social agencies in Birmingham, and evaluation of the experiences gained; (5) Religions and Ideologies: a choice between a number of options, including Hinduism, Islam, Primal Religion, Buddhism, Secularism and Marxism; (6) Situation and Area Studies: Africa, Asia, Latin America, the Caribbean and Europe; (7) Community Development, an introduction to what is being done by governments and other agencies towards the betterment of communities in underprivileged areas with a view to understanding the responsibility of the Church for involvement in social change.

The pattern is repeated each fortnight, and offers a wide variety of options to the student, while retaining an essential common core. Over twenty staff members are engaged in the semester, each bringing his or her own specialism to bear on a concerted programme. The groups are carefully selected, ensuring a cross-section of nationality, denomination, cultural and educational background, though for certain purposes those with similar interests and aptitudes meet together. Undergirding the course of study is the community life of the different colleges which are themselves international and ecumenical, even though a particular denomination may be the sponsoring body. There may be anything up to twenty different nationalities in one college and several confessional backgrounds. All of this enriches the worship and common life, and students learn to adjust to the unfamiliar and build relationships with those who are very different from themselves.

As I have said, the training programme in Christian mission is still in its early and experimental stages. It is already exhibiting its tensions and teething troubles, but advisory and steering committees of staff and students keep it under constant review. Changes will undoubtedly be made in the light of experience, and different options, such as urban and industrial mission, will probably be introduced in the future. Nor is anyone satisfied with the degree of engagement so far achieved in the complex world of a great Midland city, with its racial tensions and jungle of social problems. But at any rate a start has been made in trying to come to grips with the sort of training required for the ministry and mission of the Church in the world of today.

The course at Selly Oak could serve as the framework for a final period of training for selected theological students from a variety of colleges. Indeed this is already beginning to happen, though, with rare exceptions apart from those going overseas, they have so far come from abroad: from Asia and Africa, from Europe and North America, returning to their own countries to engage in mission there. However, if it makes sense for them, it should make no less sense for British students. Mission is indivisible.

The experiment I have just described is cited merely as an example of the way in which training for the ministry may begin to be redirected. Taken by itself, it is only a drop in the bucket. The problem, when viewed as a whole, is of immense proportions. This becomes increasingly apparent when we begin to realize that education for ministry in a changing world has to be a continuing process. Is it possible any longer to be content with pre-ordination training in the blithe belief that this will equip a man for a lifetime of service? Already there are stirrings not only at the grass roots, but also in the tree tops. Refresher courses are being mooted and on a very limited scale are now being arranged. But here again patchwork tinkering will not meet the case. As the Principal of William Temple College argued at a recent consultation, a massive change of strategy is required: the Church will have to face a reordering of priorities and a redeployment of resources, curtailing the emphasis on pre-ordination training and providing opportunities for continuing in-service education.

All of this points to a ferment of discussion in the days ahead. Indeed, it has already begun. The report of the commission of the World Council of Churches on theological education makes that abundantly plain. The death knell of the small denominational college has been sounded. The question is how long it will wait for burial and what will take its place.

Chapter Six

Radical Faith

So far very little has been said about the major, and indeed fundamental, crisis confronting the Church today: the crisis of faith. There is no point in talking about revolutionizing the structures of the Church and exploring new patterns of ministry if Christians do not know what to believe and have no gospel to which they are committed. And here, it must be confessed, confusion reigns.

Buffeted by the winds of change and the radical criticism to which the Christian faith is being subjected, the Church is in grave danger of losing its nerve, either by retreating into traditional orthodoxy and giving up the struggle to come to terms with the questions of the modern world, or else by surrendering to the argument that this is no time for theological reconstruction: we must simply be content to take soundings in the expectation that they will lead to a more adequate restatement of the Gospel in the days ahead.[1] In my view, neither of these alternatives is necessary. I believe that it is possible to interpret the historic faith in a secular age without abandoning its clarity or cutting edge, provided that we are prepared to be ruthlessly critical of our presuppositions and do not make pretentious claims for our dogmatic formulations. What is required is not a destructive radicalism but a return to the roots, a real radicalism, an uncovering of the essence of the unchanging Gospel.

In the compass of this concluding chapter I can do no more

than set up four signposts to what I believe to be the basic issues with which we have to come to terms: (1) recovery of belief in God; (2) the predicament of man; (3) the role of Jesus; (4) the Christian hope in a revolutionary age.

1. At the core of the modern crisis of faith is the possibility of meaningful belief in God. The crisis is much more serious than it has ever been in the past. Throughout history there have been disputes about the truth of particular doctrines; but today it is the reality of God himself that is in question, not only from sceptics outside the Church, but from theologians within it. The roots of all this are to be traced back to the Renaissance and to the writings of Immanuel Kant and David Hume, who may with justification be called the fathers of modern empirical philosophy and its sometimes cavalier dismissal of metaphysics as the impossible attempt to go beyond the data presented in sense experience. It this conclusion is well founded, then it renders all talk of the supernatural highly problematical and 'God' becomes an unintelligible word. The full consequences of eighteenth-century scepticism have been worked out in recent decades first by the early Logical Positivists and later by their successors, the Logical Analysts, and it is against this background that 'the new theology' has been developed. Popularized by the Bishop of Woolwich in *Honest to God*,[2] it has been given more radical expression by such writers as Paul Van Buren, Alfred Starratt, Harvey Cox and Ronald Gregor Smith,[3] and has reached its zenith or nadir, according to one's point of view, in the 'death of God' theology of Thomas J. Altizer and William Hamilton.[4] Thus the attempt has been made to interpret Christian belief to fit in with a framework of thought which rejects the traditional categories of theism. As Leslie Paul points

out, that has meant throwing everything into the melting pot:

> For nearly two thousand years Christianity has lived with a certain frame of reference, which in part it drew from Judaism . . . The new theology and the 'death of God' theology put the whole frame of reference under question. If there is no God in independence, then what is meant by God is problematical, and what is meant by incarnation possibly nonsensical . . . From theology at its most extreme we face the prospect of the dissolution of the Christian faith as received not only from the centuries but from the Gospels and Epistles; hence the phrase Christian atheism.[5]

Whilst I believe as firmly as anyone that it is our inescapable responsibility to re-examine and reinterpret the Christian Faith in the light of all the knowledge available to us, I am persuaded that the new theologians are leading us up the garden path, or, to use a more appropriate metaphor, into the heart of a tangled jungle. I say this in full recognition of the immensely valuable contribution they have made in stimulating thought and awakening the Church out of its dogmatic slumbers. But to take as an axiom that metaphysics and supernaturalism belong to an age that is past seems to me to be a quite unwarrantable assumption. In the first place, it is important to distinguish between the scientific and philosophical presuppositions which lie behind the conclusions that are drawn; and in the writings of the new theologians they are often confused. On strictly scientific grounds there is no justification for the limiting assumption to which I have referred. For the natural scientist in his professional capacity the question of metaphysics does not arise, still less the legitimacy or otherwise of thinking about God as supernatural. He is concerned with a restricted field of enquiry and with the abstraction of certain aspects of that field which are amenable to controlled experimentation. The scientific method neither precludes nor does it directly suggest any metaphysical or theological account of the universe. Such issues lie outside the realm of experimental science, which, properly understood, is completely neutral in respect to them.

However, the rejection of metaphysics and supernaturalism by certain contemporary theologians seems ultimately to turn on the assumption that modern philosophy has made such a procedure inescapable. I find this quite astonishing. Its *naïveté* is exposed by the mere mention of names like Brand Blanshard, Charles Hartshorne and John E. Smith in the United States or C. A. Campbell, J. N. Findlay and H. D. Lewis on this side of the Atlantic, all of whom are philosophers of international repute, fully persuaded that metaphysics is far from outmoded (indeed, it would be difficult to find a more thorough-going metaphysical treatise than Findlay's recent Gifford Lectures[6]). These distinguished scholars do, of course, differ from one another, and their views are often highly controversial; but they represent a wide conspectus of contemporary philosophical thought of which many modern theologians hardly seem to be aware. Even when we turn to those who would claim to stand firmly in the empirical tradition, we find an openness to metaphysical questions which was not the case a generation ago. Much water has flowed beneath the bridge since the early Logical Positivists declared that the only meaningful statements, other than those of mathematics and formal logic, were propositions verifiable in sense experience, and that since metaphysical and theological statements were not verifiable in this way they were to be dubbed as nonsensical. This is a philosophical position which has been steadily losing ground for the last thirty years, and those who stand within the positivist-analytic tradition are far more cautious in their strictures these days than were their much more confident predecessors.[7]

Accordingly there could scarcely be anything more cavalier than Starratt's summary dismissal of the concept of God as supernatural on the ground that this is unacceptable 'in terms of modern standards of verification'. And the narrowness of his frame of reference is further underlined when he adds: 'Men educated in our culture are taught to accept as knowledge only those propositions which are derived from sensory experience of the kind that can be repeated by any trained observer. Whether a laboratory technician or not, the educated man of our time is an empiricist. . . .'[8] Such statements as this betray no hint of suspicion that empiricism may itself raise metaphysical questions, nor the least recognition that many philosophers, who are fully cognizant of all that has been happening over the past few decades, have subjected any arbitrarily delimited empiricism to devastating criticism.

In short, it is not, I believe, going too far to say that some of the new theologians, who are exercising such widespread influence with their claim to be reinterpreting belief in God in terms of modern thought, are themselves sadly out of date. The fundamental questions about the nature of reality are as open as ever they were. Needless to say, this does not imply that philosophical enquiry is necessarily favourable to any particular metaphysical theory, still less to any kind of theism. My point is simply that it is unwarrantable to accept a passing fashion in philosophy as a fixed framework within which to reformulate the Christian Faith, especially when the fashion itself is outdated.

If, then, we are liberated from our inhibitions, can we begin to think significantly about God as the Creator and Lord of the universe? I believe that we can, as we expose ourselves to the dimension of mystery pervading the whole natural order. Throughout history man's religious experience has been grounded in his apprehension of a Presence transcending and yet involved in the world of which he is part. For many of our contemporaries, as Dorothy Sayers once said in an unpublished letter, 'the dimension we call God is missing'. But because many miss it and live by surface acquaintance, this does not alter the fact that there is a dimension of reality to which poets, artists, musicians, mystics and countless simple people have borne witness down the centuries. This, they would claim, is not just the experience of the natural order in depth. Nor is it the crude projection of an image of the God 'up there' or 'out there' or 'down under'. As the Archbishop of Canterbury so pointedly says, it is not a question of spatially locating God, but of insisting that he is *different from* the natural order, yet apprehended through it.[9]

The elucidation and interpretation of this experience are the business of natural theology, a discipline sorely neglected in recent years. The Church is now paying a heavy price for the influence of Karl Barth who, despite his outstanding contribution to Christian thought and the necessary corrective he gave to the liberalism of his early days, persuaded a whole generation that philosophical enquiry had nothing to offer to man's understanding of God and that natural theology was a blind alley. This has been compounded by many of the new theologians who, as Nathaniel Micklem wittily remarked in my hearing, have become so absorbed in the city, in its skyscrapers, its blocks of flats and its factories, man's achievements through his development of technology, 'that they appear to have lost all touch with nature except for occasional visits to the greengrocer'. The great British tradition of natural theology, represented by such giants of the past as Clement Webb, John Oman and William Temple, urgently needs to be recovered, though it will obviously have to take into account all that has happened in the intervening years. This is not to be understood as a plea to put the clock back, but rather as an invitation to look in a fresh direction, abandoning the shallows in which we now flounder. Belief in God, the transcendent Creator and Lord, is the indispensable foundation for the renewal of faith.

2. If the new theology has landed us in confusion about the reality of God, it is no less open to criticism in what it says about man. The confident assertion that man has come of age in the twentieth century sounds strange, to say the very least, against the background of the kind of world in which we are living. The intended meaning of the phrase is plain. The process of secularization has increasingly removed political and social institutions from religious control; society, it is said, has become desacralized, at any rate in the West, and this is spreading throughout the third world. Pockets remain, and bastions of the old order have still to fall; but by and large man now sees himself as in control of his political and social destiny, and in this sense is responsible for his own future. Add to this the enormous strides he has made in science and technology, conquering his environment and reaching out into space, and the picture

is complete: man has come of age, the master of his own destiny.

But that is not the whole story by a very long way. While man has made spectacular progress in subduing nature and harnessing its resources, he has not succeeded in mastering himself. Human relationships are in a mess, whether we take the large canvas of the international scene or the smaller canvas of different societies or the still smaller canvas of fellow-workers, acquaintances, friends and families. We may have claimed that political and social institutions are now our responsibility and not subject to divine sovereignty, but we have not been conspicuously successful in shaping them to rational ends. Vietnam, Biafra, Rhodesia, South Africa, the Middle East, all serve to highlight the unresolved conflicts between the Great Powers. Racial tension threatens the whole fabric of American society and is becoming a crucial issue in Britain and elsewhere. Industrial unrest is evidence of suspicion and hostility between employer and employee. Violence stalks the streets and crime is on the increase. Confrontation is the watchword of militant students. Family life is breaking down in many places. Men and women do not know how to live with one another; and for many the devastating comment of one of Sartre's characters is only too true: '*L'enfer, c'est les Autres*' ('Hell is other people').[10] Overshadowing the whole human scene is the alienation of the rich from the poor: the deepening chasm of the twentieth century.

Of course there is another side to the picture, as I have already indicated: a great fund of generosity, kindliness and goodwill lightens an otherwise dark canvas. But it does not justify us in minimizing the extent or gravity of the human problem. Man has not come of age in the sense that he has shown himself capable of handling himself and his relationships. He is an adolescent, who is at war with himself and with others; and, in spite of all pretensions to the contrary, he is exposed by what he manifestly is, by the way he lives, by his failure to forge harmonious relationships, as lacking the inward resources for full maturity. In plain speech, he needs a Saviour.

That is to introduce an unpopular word with many of our contemporaries. To say that we cannot rescue ourselves is an affront to human pride. To declare that man is a sinner, bound up with a sinful race, is to bring back the terminology of an age which many moderns have claimed to leave behind. While it is clearly important that we should pay full heed to those, like Bonhoeffer, who insist that Christianity should be addressed to man's strength, to his courage, to his sense of responsibility and to his capacity for adventure (an emphasis sadly muted, if not totally neglected, in many confessional formulations), there is an equal danger of imbalance in the other direction. The result is a superficial portrayal of man's true condition. The late Russell Maltby made the point when a modern version of the hymn 'Just as I am, without one plea' was proposed for inclusion in the Revised Methodist Hymnal. Instead of references to sin and redemption, the new version ran:

> Just as I am, young, strong and free,
> To be the best that I can be
> For truth, and righteousness, and Thee,
> Lord of my life, I come.

Maltby said he would agree to its inclusion if he were allowed to write a final verse:

Just as I am, but not like those
Who mourn their sins and tell their woes.
We turn our tails up, not our toes.
Hop, skip and jump, we come.

Man is summoned to responsible living, to the dedication of all his powers to the service of God; but at the same time he is enmeshed in the world-wide web of human selfishness, cruelty, intolerance and lust. He deludes himself if he thinks he can be free of it by his own unaided efforts; and delusion in this respect can be highly dangerous. The Archbishop of Canterbury unerringly puts his finger on a major weakness in the so-called secular theologians when he criticizes Harvey Cox for his neglect of the doctrine of grace.[11] The Pauline confession, 'All have sinned and fall short of the glory of God',[12] is amply attested in the pages of human history and is decisively confirmed by the state of the world in our own day. Has man come of age? In certain limited respects, yes. But basically, left to himself, he remains an adolescent; a dangerous adolescent both to himself and to his fellows until he finds a source of grace beyond himself. Maturity lies in the redemption of man's weakness by a power not his own, the harnessing of the limited strength he has to offer to the fullness of God's grace.

3. That brings us to the central figure of the New Testament. 'You shall call his name Jesus, for he will save his people from their sins.'[13] So he is designated in the prologue to St Matthew's Gospel. A whole library of books has been written about the titles attributed to Jesus: Son of God, Son of Man, Messiah, Suffering Servant, Saviour, Great High Priest, Lord. Controversy has ranged over the meaning of these titles as well as over the question how far

they were claimed, explicitly or implicitly, by Jesus himself and how far they were attributed to him by his disciples and by the early Church. By common consent the confession 'Jesus is Lord'[14] belongs to the most primitive substratum of tradition, but even this, as Michael Ramsey points out, was not free from ambiguity. 'It could mean one with sovereign power, with little more explicit definition. It could mean the Messiah. It could mean—in the context of the Greek cults—the Lord of a mystery religion. It could recall the title used in the worship of the Roman Emperor, *dominus noster*. It could mean, to readers of the Greek Old Testament, the LORD God of the Bible.'[15] Similarly with all the other designations. 'Every title used in revelation can mislead as well as reveal, for no words are adequate for the revelation. It is in the history of their use that their transcendent significance is seen.'[16]

By the last sentence I take Ramsey to mean that all the titles attributed to Jesus point to the mystery of his Person as this was impressed upon the disciples and those who believed in him through their testimony. It was the attempt to express the ultimately inexpressible, to reflect facets of what he was and what he had done with the most appropriate categories ready to hand. In this connexion it does not matter whether Jesus claimed the titles for himself or whether they were attributed to him by his followers, though in so far as the former was the case they would obviously carry that much greater authority. But on either supposition the titles are signposts, pointing with different degrees of significance to that ineffable personality whose influence on his contemporaries and subsequent generations has moulded the course of events ever since.

When, therefore, we ask who Jesus was and what is his

continuing role in the pageant of history, the confusion of our own times and the ultimate destiny of the universe, we have to look beyond the titles attributed to him and beyond the credal formulations and confessions, which at best can serve as signposts, to a reality they cannot possibly fully expose. This is a lesson which has not been generally deduced from the work of the Form Critics: those who have argued that the New Testament documents represent the faith of the early Church enshrined in recognizable forms, and that it is impossible to arrive at an objective picture of the historical Jesus, who is hidden from us behind the screen of the theological reflection and the apologetic interest of those living in the latter half of the first century A.D. Even if we were to accept this conclusion without qualification, it would not follow that we were left with a superstructure without foundation and could confidently dismiss the New Testament as originating in the subjective imagination of the credulous. I recall a conversation when I was a student with the late Professor R. H. Lightfoot, one of the early pioneers of Form Criticism. He maintained that it was a complete misunderstanding of his position to suppose that it implied an attenuated picture of Jesus. On the contrary, he maintained, the actual Person must at the very least have been of a stature sufficient to sustain the beliefs which came to centre round him. So far from this controversial approach resulting in reducing the figure of Jesus to a shadow, Lightfoot contended that we had to come to terms with One who transcended all the theological formulations and confessions of faith attributable either to the early Church or to subsequent generations.

Over the past thirty years the negative conclusions of the earlier Form Critics have increasingly come under serious question and the contention has been gaining ground that scepticism about knowing anything of the actual life of Jesus is unwarranted. 'I cannot believe,' writes Donald Baillie, 'that there is any good reason for the defeatism of those who gave up all hope of penetrating the tradition and reaching an assured knowledge of the historical personality of Jesus. Surely such defeatism is a transient nightmare of Gospel criticism, from which we are now awakening to a more sober confidence in our quest for the Jesus of history.'[17] This seems to me to be a well-founded judgement and, if accepted, it is obviously of crucial importance; for it gives more definite content to our apprehension of Jesus as he presented himself to his contemporaries. But in the last resort, however close we can get to the testimony of eye-witnesses, we are left with the impression that Jesus made on those who were acquainted with him, and that cannot possibly exhaust the reality which he incarnated. As I argued in a previous chapter, the truth with which we are confronted as embodied in the person of Jesus transcends the truth of anything that can be thought or said about him.[18]

My own conclusion, then, is this: behind the record of the New Testament stands one who was a numinous personality, who convinced his disciples that God was in some way meeting them in him. 'He taught them as one who had authority, and not as the scribes.'[19] 'No man ever spoke like this man!'[20] He declared the forgiveness of sins. He announced the advent of God's kingdom through his own actions. He made such an impression on Simon that he cried out, 'Depart from me, for I am a sinful man, O Lord.'[21] And when the soldiers and officers of the chief priests came to arrest him in the Garden of Gethsemane, the author of the Fourth Gospel records that, on his acknowledgment '"I am he," they drew back and fell to the ground.'[22] This does not leave us with a shadowy figure, a mere X without content,[23] but with one whose stature was so overwhelming that it defies all attempts to delimit it within human categories.

Furthermore, our picture of Jesus is not restricted to what he was. The mystery of his person is primarily disclosed in what he did. As Bultmann said of theology in general, it 'cannot speak of God as he is in himself, but only of what he does for us'.[24] This was where the early Christians took their stand. They had been delivered from their bondage to sin and death; they had been reconciled to God and had found one another in a community which transcended every barrier of sex, class, race and nation. They claimed that they owed this to Jesus, to what he had accomplished by his death and resurrection whereby a new age had been inaugurated—the age of the kingdom. There can be no doubt that for them the life into which they had entered was due to him, and to him alone. What he had done and what he continued to do were the source and ground of their new experience; and in his actions they discerned the direct activity of God.

The precise relation of the event to the experience has defied human understanding, in spite of all the theories of the atonement that have been propounded down the centuries. They draw their inspiration from a variety of models, all to be found in the New Testament: the sacrificial worship of Israel, the slave market, the court of law, the military conquest and the family. But in the end, while every model throws light upon the cross, none of them nor all of them taken together can exhaust the depth of God's great act of reconciliation. It has been one of the most disastrous causes of division amongst Christians when one of these models has been elevated into being an exclusive definition of what took place. As R. W. Dale once said, 'It is not the doctrine of the death of Christ that atones for human sin, but the death itself.'[25]

This may seem very remote to those of us living in the second half of the twentieth century, immersed in the practical affairs of today. The events of which the New Testament speaks occurred nearly two thousand years ago in an insignificant part of the Roman Empire, in a world quite different from our own, in a climate of thought utterly alien to the modern scientific and technological age. It is a problem not only of distance in time, but of an apparent lack of contact with the realities of contemporary living; the theological concepts and language used to interpret the cross and resurrection strike so many as abstract and theoretical, unrelated to the hard facts of everyday existence. How can they come alive today for those on the factory floor, in the offices and the shops, on the stock exchange, in hospitals, schools and colleges, in government departments and welfare agencies, in the inner city, in suburbia and in the countryside? What has all this theology got to do with life as it is?

The answer, I believe, lies in the impact of ordinary Christian men and women: those who down the centuries and in our own time have claimed that all that they are and all that they hope to be are rooted and grounded in their faith in Christ crucified, risen and ascended. The Church is one of the most popular whipping boys. Its institutional image has been widely decried and its members have been castigated for hypocrisy, pomposity and sheer failure to live up to the standards they profess. Much of the criticism is justified and accepted with shame and contrition; much is unfair, highly generalized and reflects on the critics themselves, who often appear ignorant, complacent and unwarrantably supercilious. But when everything adverse has been said that can be said, the fact remains that there are countless ordinary Christians whose lives constitute an inescapable challenge to the self-satisfied, the defeated and the bewildered of our generation. They are the salt of the earth and the light of the world, and this not because of anything they would claim for themselves, but because they acknowledge that they owe everything to what Christ has done for them and in them.

As I write these lines, I think of some of those whom I have been privileged to know and who have been a constant reminder in days of doubt and questioning of the things that cannot be shaken. One such example is that of a former church officer whose grace of character has consistently made a profound impression on all those who have had anything to do with him. Having received nothing more than an elementary education, he worked as a labourer until his retirement, and now, nearing ninety years of age, he possesses that rarest of gifts—a serene inner tranquillity which is the fruit of a lifetime of devoted Christian discipleship in the service of others. No one will ever reckon on earth how much good he has done; mere hints have been given by stories told of visits to those in trouble, nights spent in the homes of the sick and dying, simple acts of kindness done without prompting on anyone's part. He has never achieved anything spectacular nor has his name ever appeared in the newspapers; he has chaired no important committee and launched no great cause; but in terms of constructive human relationships I have not known his equal. Young and old instinctively trust him; teenagers have sought him out as an understanding friend; and at the end of his life he finds himself beloved by a whole community. The most attractive thing about him is his genuine unpretentiousness; he would be astonished to the point of bewilderment to know that he had been singled out as an example of one who mirrors the Christ in whom his life is grounded.

It would be a grievous mistake to conclude that I have simply chosen an example of other-worldly pietism. I could have mentioned an outstanding public figure, like Martin Luther King, whose contribution to human welfare and social justice has captured the imagination of countless people. But concentration on the dramatic and spectacular can all too easily obscure the fact that a man does not need to be endowed with extraordinary gifts or to be in a position of exercising widespread influence to leave his mark on the lives of others. The unheralded saint who does justice, loves mercy and walks humbly with his God may have accomplished something of no less importance than those who deservedly catch the public eye.

Whoever they may be, amongst the notable or the ordinary according to this world's standards, those who claim to live by the power of the Cross and the Resurrection present evidence that has to be explained or explained away. If they are deluded, then the finest flower of human personality is without firm roots. This I find it impossible to believe. Although I gladly acknowledge that there are many wise and good men and women who make no religious profession and are indeed better than a lot of Christians, I have yet to meet amongst them any who match the distinctive quality of a life profoundly grounded in the grace of God in Jesus Christ. I can only say that in my experience this is *sui generis*. As a young army officer remarked during the Second World War: 'I can dispute all the Christian doctrines, but I cannot argue about the lives of some of the Christians I have known.' The most powerful testimony to who Christ was is to be found in those who claim to owe everything to him.

4. There is one further subject on which I wish to touch: the Christian attitude to the future. This is largely an age without hope, or, where hope is cherished, more often than not it takes a desperate form. The old liberal idea of inevitable progress is virtually dead, and, apart from a few starry-eyed optimists, the Marxist vision of the future has received shattering blows as a result of political events in the Communist world. Where hope is fervently kept alive it inspires the philosophy of violent revolution, though for those who embrace it the destruction of the existing system is a far clearer objective than anything positive to take its place. As for religion, most people regard it as bound to the past, and when it speaks of the future, as in Christianity, it seems to do so in incredible pictures drawn from a pre-scientific age, predicting a cosmic catastrophe which sounds more like doom than triumph. Most people give up thinking about the future altogether, clinging to the vanishing present as the only reality which has any meaning for them.

In this situation Christians need to recover their conviction as to the fulfilment of God's purpose for the whole created universe. The Gospel, though rooted in the past, is oriented to the future, and the future breaking into the present as the guarantee of what is to come. St Paul speaks of the birth of a new creation in Christ, a new humanity focused in him, to be consummated in the reconciliation of the entire cosmos. This is not simply a dream of the distant future. The apostle declares that it is already manifest: 'If any one is in Christ, he is a new creation; the old has passed away, behold, the new has come.'[26] From the purely human standpoint mankind does not exist; it is an abstraction. We live in our communities, separated from one another by the barriers of race, nation, class, and personal prejudice and predilection. Jesus is the focus of a new universal humanity. He is the Son of Man, understood in a representative and corporate sense, by whose life, death and resurrection the old order has been superseded and the promise of a recreated humanity offered to men in the here and now. As Father McCabe says in his penetrating exposition of the theme: 'Jesus is the future destiny of mankind (to which we are summoned by the Father) trying to be present among men in our present age. He offers a new way in which men can be together, a new way in which they can be free to be themselves, the way of total self-giving, and he offers this amongst the various makeshift ways in which men have tried to build community.'[27] In him the future has invaded the present with the real possibility that all things can become new.

To many this may sound like abstract theology. We live in a divided world, torn by strife and riddled with factions. We have to come to terms with things as they are, not with things as we would like them to be. To speak of Christ as the focus of a new mankind is to talk of an ideal, whereas we have to accommodate ourselves to the grim facts.

The objection is one that obviously has some substance to it. Nevertheless it ignores the claim that those who are in Christ *are* the new creation in spite of being part of the old order at the same time. In other words, Christians belong to two worlds, inevitably experiencing the tension that this implies. St Paul spoke of the Corinthians as those 'upon whom the end of the ages has come',[28] or, to use Father Lionel Thornton's vivid translation, 'those who live in the overlap of the ages'.[29] Their feet were still upon this earth, but their perspective was from above.

This belonging to two worlds is graphically illustrated in C. S. Lewis's *Pilgrim's Regress*, in which a boy called John sets out to search for the beautiful island he had glimpsed in childhood as he looked through a hole in the wall near his home. After wandering through many different cities and villages and talking to many people, he reaches an impassable canyon. Failing to find a way across on his own, he allows himself to be conducted to the far side, and so by dint of many adventures finally arrives at the seashore in company with a host of others. There, across the water, he sees the island of his dreams with the towering mountains behind. 'Pray, do we take a ship from here?' he asks his guide. 'No' is the reply. Surely he is aware of the elementary fact that the earth is round. So John is told that he must retrace his steps and return to his point of departure, reaching the island by way of the mountains. ' "Come," said the Guide at last, "if you are ready let us start East again. But I should warn you of one thing—the country will look very different on the return journey." '[30]

Pilgrim's regress. Christians travel the same road as those who make no such profession, but their perspective is different; they live in the overlap of the ages. But there is more to it than that. Not only do they have a different perspective; they are committed to the transformation of the old world by the invasion of the new. It is not just that they see things from another standpoint; they are summoned to believe that the world is being recreated in the light of the heavenly vision, and that they are privileged to share in the new creation.

This does not mean, as the so-called secular theologians seem to suggest, that this world is the only sphere of God's activity or man's involvement. If this world is being re-created in the light of the heavenly vision, then it is only in the perspective of an eternal order beyond the death of the individual and the end of the historical process that the transformation of everything has any ultimate Christian foundation. The words of the apostle still stand: 'If for this life only we have hoped in Christ, we are of all men most to be pitied.'[31] So far, however, from belief in the eternal context landing us in other-worldliness, it is the indispensable prerequisite for having any hope for the world in which we now live.

Here is the seed of a theology of revolution. Christians are not condemned to 'pie in the sky' as an escape from the grim realities of conditions as they are. Nor are they committed to some facile utopianism, believing that they can build the kingdom of God by their own efforts. On the contrary, they are summoned to identify themselves with God's revolutionary activity, whereby he anticipates the kingdom of heaven, the fulfilment of his purpose to reconcile all things in Christ. This means identification with the future, not with the past. It is not the product of evolution, but of revolution, the breaking into the present of a new order; and the good news of the kingdom is that it is here, even though its fulfilment awaits the end of time. 'As it is, we do not yet see everything in subjection to him. But we see Jesus . . . crowned with glory and honour.'[32]

The relationship between this radical Christian revolution

and the secular revolutionary movements of our time is inevitably problematic. In the latter McCabe sees types of the Christian commitment to the death of the old order and resurrection to the new. To quote his own words, 'every revolution which deals with structures less ultimate than this is an image of, and a preparation for, the resurrection of the dead. The Cuban and Vietnamese revolution is a type of the resurrection in the sense that we speak of Old Testament events as types of Christ.'[33] This striking comparison compels us to face the reality of what is actually happening in the world today. Wherever there is revolt against poverty, oppression and injustice, wherever men stand up to be counted in the struggle for the dignity of man and a universal human community, there are the signs of the kingdom. But they may be ambiguous signs, or signs which may be obscured altogether by the corruption of human idealism. There is all the world of difference between the new humanity in Christ grounded in the gospel of reconciliation and a secular order in which the strong dominate the weak and impose their will on others.

Thus in the modern revolutionary age Christians find themselves in a difficult position. Living in the world as it is, but committed to its radical transformation, they are called to stand with Christ in the rejection of the old order of exploitation and hostility and in alignment with all those who are committed to its overthrow. At the same time they are compelled to oppose all revolution that is not based on reconciliation, maintaining that hatred and envy, violence and oppression, so far from being justifiable on pragmatic grounds, are destructive of any community worth achieving.

Here is a straight choice confronting those of every age. If the old order is under condemnation, what is the new order to take its place? Is it the distant hope of an international, inter-racial and classless society achieved by the elimination of all who stand in its way and the domination of a self-righteous few, corrupted by their own idealism? Or is it the new humanity in Christ, given here and now, wherever men and women put themselves at the disposal of his reconciling power? It is the task of the Church to present the latter alternative as a living option, particularly for the rising generation.

This chapter is not intended to be a conspectus of Christian belief but, as I have said, my purpose has been to indicate four signposts to the radical convictions which Christians need to hold if there is to be any point in talking about the renewal of the Church. Unless we believe in God as other than ourselves and the universe of which we are part, the very basis for Christianity is lacking. Unless we come to terms with man as lost without the grace of God, we shall be living in a world of make-believe. Unless we are persuaded that God has disclosed himself in Jesus as Saviour and Lord, we lose touch with all that is distinctively Christian and abandon the very foundation for evangelism. And unless we can recover hope for the future which is firmly grounded in the eternal order and at the same time clearly related to the world as it is, we shall have nothing to say to this generation in its perplexity and despair. Many other aspects of Christian belief call for fresh examination and elucidation. But it is a waste of time to prune the tree if you have decided to cut away its roots. Only when the Church has recovered its nerve by coming to grips once more with the heart of its faith can it declare, 'Now is the acceptable time; behold, now is the day of salvation.'[34]

Notes

Chapter One

1. John 1: 14.
2. A. E. Whitham, *The Discipline and Culture of the Spiritual Life* (London, Hodder and Stoughton, 1938), p. 32.
3. Phil. 2: 7.
4. John 1: 6.
5. Matt. 11: 28 (NEB).
6. Monica Furlong, *With Love to the Church* (London, Hodder and Stoughton, 1965), p. 21.
7. John 14: 6.
8. 1 Cor. 13: 12 (NEB).
9. Cf. A. J. Ayer, *The Concept of a Person and Other Essays* (London, Macmillan, 1963), pp. 181–5.
10. John Oman, *Grace and Personality* (Cambridge, University Press, 1925), p. 70.
11. Gal. 5: 22–3.
12. E.g. Matt. 7: 21.
13. Matt. 15: 18.
14. James 2: 17.
15. Matt. 7: 18.
16. Cf. Joseph Fletcher, *Moral Responsibility* (London, SCM, 1967).
17. 2 Cor. 5: 19.
18. Eph. 4: 13.
19. Cf. *Putting Asunder* (London, SPCK, 1966), the report of a commission on divorce set up by the Archbishop of Canterbury, in which the inescapability of a double standard was

acknowledged. The members of the Commission began by recognizing that the Church is committed to the ideal of life-long partnership as a sacramental bond, whereas this should not be imposed by law upon those who are not prepared to accept Christian suppositions. Accordingly, they set themselves the task of advising the Archbishop as to the way in which the law could be reformed to allow for this distinction.

20. Heb. 11: 10.
21. David L. Edwards, *Religion and Change* (London, Hodder and Stoughton, 1969), p. 51.
22. Matt. 9: 36 (NEB).
23. Rom. 12: 2.

Chapter Two

1. Werner Krusche, 'Parish Structure—A Hindrance to Mission', H. T. Neve (Ed.), in *Sources for Change* (Geneva, World Council of Churches, 1968).
2. Ibid., p. 55.
3. Cf. *New Christian* (21 September 1967), p. 8.
4. Matt. 23: 24.
5. Milton, *Areopagitica* (London, Effingham Wilson, 1840), p. 39.
6. Harvey Cox, *The Secular City* (London, SCM, 1965), p. 161.
7. This is rendered all the more inescapable by the settlement of large numbers of immigrants, coming from the so-called mission fields, in many of our big cities. It is an obvious anomaly when a Missionary Society claims to have responsibility in Pakistan, but not for Pakistanis in this country.
8. *Church of England Year Book* (London, SPCK, 1967), pp. 285–99.
9. A Baptist minister recently remarked that it cost more to stoke the boiler than to maintain himself and his family!
10. Leslie Paul, *The Deployment and Payment of the Clergy* (London, Church Information Office, 1964).

11. Leslie Paul, *The Death and Resurrection of the Church* (London, Hodder and Stoughton, 1968), pp. 56 f.
12. Proposals to deal with the problems of the parson's freehold and patronage have been made in the report by W. Fenton-Morley, *Partners in Ministry* (London, Church Information Office, 1967). For a critical appraisal, see Leslie Paul, *The Death and Resurrection of the Church*, pp. 62–5.
13. Ibid., pp. 111–13.
14. At the same time, we should not minimize the striking percentage of the population who claim adherence to Christianity, even if they never or rarely attend church. Cf. David Martin, *A Sociology of English Religion* (London, Heinemann, 1967).
15. Gibson Winter, *The Suburban Captivity of the Churches* (New York, Doubleday, 1961).
16. It is, of course, possible to overstate this case and ignore the influence of suburbia in an age of growing affluence and leisure. Cf. David L. Edwards, *Religion and Change*, pp. 87 and 102.
17. Winter, op. cit., p. 129.

Chapter Three

1. Matt. 16: 18.
2. The sermon is not in print, but the theme is one to which Canon Taylor has frequently returned in his newsletters and elsewhere. See, for example, *For All the World* (Philadelphia Westminster Press, 1966), pp. 48–60.
3. Heb. 11: 8.
4. Matt. 8: 20.
5. Herbert McCabe, *Law, Love and Language* (London, Sheed and Ward, 1968), pp. 123 ff.
6 *Unity Begins at Home* (London, SCM, 1964), p. 79.
7. Ibid., p. 78.
8. R. M. C. Jeffery, *Areas of Ecumenical Experiment* (London British Council of Churches, 1968).

9. Neville Cryer, *Parishes with a Purpose* (London, Mowbray, 1967), p. 53. A more complete account of the Desborough experiment is given here (pp. 41–58).
10. The memorandum of the Bishop of Oxford is quoted in full by Jeffery, op. cit., pp. 66–8.
11. The text is to be found in Jeffery, op. cit., pp. 59–65.
12. Ibid., p. 59.
13. Ibid., p. 61.
14. Ibid., p. 62.
15. Ibid., p. 60.
16. Neville Cryer and Ernest Goodridge, *Experiment in Unity* (London, Mowbray, 1968).
17. The Roman Catholics took their full share of the expenses from the outset, and the Baptists made a donation at a later stage after initial hesitation.
18. Cf. Roger Lloyd, *The Church of England, 1900–1965* (London, SCM, 1966), pp. 530–5.
19. Cf. Neville Cryer, *Parishes with a Purpose*, pp. 27–40.
20. E. W. Southcott, *The Parish Comes Alive* (London, Mowbray, 1956), p. 60.
21. Ibid., p. 63.
22. Ibid., p. 127.
23. Ibid., p. 58.
24. John V. Taylor, *Change of Address* (London, Hodder and Stoughton, 1968), pp. 121–42.
25. *A New Way*, explanatory leaflet of the Notting Hill Ecumenical Centre.
26. *Intercommunion Today* (London, Church Information Office, 1968).
27. Ibid., p. 122.
28. Ibid., p. 127.
29. Ibid., p. 128.
30. Cryer and Goodridge, *Experiment in Unity*, p. 20.
31. Isaiah 28: 10.

32. *Unity Begins at Home*, p. 78.
33. William McSweeney, *New Christian* (8 August 1968), pp. 19–20.

Chapter Four

1. Leslie Paul, *The Death and Resurrection of the Church*, p. 86.
2. Colin W. Williams, *The Church* (Philadelphia, Westminster Press, 1968), pp. 161 ff.
3. *Anglican-Methodist Unity, Part 2, The Scheme* (London, SPCK and Epworth, 1968), p. 7.
4. Graham Leonard, *To Every Man's Conscience* (privately published, 1968). Cf. Margaret Deanesly and Geoffrey C. Willis, *Anglican-Methodist Unity* (London, Faith Press, 1968).
5. Geoffrey Fisher, *The Anglican-Methodist Conversations and Problems of Church Unity* (London, OUP, 1964), pp. 41–4. Cf. his contribution to 'Anglican-Methodist Unity' in *The Church Quarterly*, vol. 1 (October 1968), pp. 119–25.
6. Cf. Richard Taylor, *New Christian* (29 December 1966 and 12 January 1967), pp. 10–11 in both issues, in which he instances Scunthorpe in Lincolnshire as the natural focus for a human zone.
7. *Cathedrals in Modern Life* (London, Church Information Office, 1961), pp. 9 f.
8. The Church Assembly has a proposal under consideration for the establishment of new dioceses, each with its centre, not necessarily a cathedral, and a central staff.
9. H. C. N. Williams, *Cathedral Reborn*, quoted by Roger Lloyd, *The Church of England, 1900–1965*, p. 568.
10. Since this paragraph was written, the Provost has announced that he is making an appeal for funds to establish a comprehensive educational programme, the scope of which will be interesting to see.
11. Cf. Gibson Winter, *The Suburban Captivity of the Churches*, p. 176.

Chapter Five

1. Gibson Winter, *The New Creation as Metropolis* (New York, Macmillan, 1963), p. 65.
2. 1 Peter 2: 9.
3. Winter, op. cit., p. 59.
4. See Weimar edition of *Luther's Works*, VI, p. 564.
5. John V. Taylor, *Change of Address*, pp. 143–59.
6. Ibid., p. 144.
7. Ibid., pp. 144 f.
8. Ibid., p. 146.
9. Eph. 4: 11.
10. Taylor, op. cit., pp. 146 f.
11. Cf. Roger Lloyd, *The Church of England, 1900–1965*, pp. 523 f. and 557 f.
12. At the same time it should be noted that some universities, like St Andrews, are beginning to introduce postgraduate diplomas in Pastoral and Social Studies which go a long way to meet the point I am making. But that still leaves open the question whether universities are the best context for such a programme or how far they will be permitted to pursue this policy in the future.
13. Taylor, op. cit., pp. 143–59.
14. Charles Fielding, 'Twenty-three Theological Schools: Aspects of Canadian Theological Education', *Canadian Journal of Theology*, XII (October 1966), pp. 229–37. For a review of recent North American studies on the subject, see Norman E. Wagner and Aarne J. Siirala, 'Fresh Approaches to Theological Education', *Canadian Journal of Theology*, XIV (July 1968), pp. 149–59.

Chapter Six

1. Cf. A. R. Vidler, ed., *Soundings, Essays concerning Christian Understanding* (Cambridge, University Press, 1962).
2. John Robinson, *Honest to God* (London, SCM, 1963).
3. Cf. Paul van Buren, *The Secular Meaning of the Gospel* (New York, Macmillan, 1963); Alfred B. Starratt, *The Real God* (London, SCM, 1965); Harvey E. Cox, *The Secular City* (London, SCM, 1965); R. Gregor Smith, *Secular Christianity* (London, Collins, 1966).
4. Cf. T. J. Altizer and William Hamilton, *Radical Theology and the Death of God* (New York, Bobbs-Merrill, 1966).
5. Leslie Paul, *The Death and Resurrection of the Church*, pp. 17 f.
6. J. N. Findlay, *The Discipline of the Cave* and *The Transcendence of the Cave* (London, Allen and Unwin, 1966–7).
7. Cf. P. F. Strawson, *Individuals: an Essay in Descriptive Metaphysics* (London, Methuen, 1959) and *Prospect for Metaphysics*, ed. Ian T. Ramsey (London, Allen and Unwin, 1961).
8. Starratt, op. cit., pp. 31 f.
9. A. M. Ramsey, *God, Christ and the World* (London, SCM, 1969).
10. Jean-Paul Sartre, *Huis Clos* (London, Methuen, 1965), p. 46.
11. Ramsey, op. cit., pp. 26–9.
12. Rom. 3: 23.
13. Matt. 1: 21.
14. 1 Cor. 12: 3.
15. Ramsey, op. cit., p. 92.
16. Ibid., p. 93.
17. Donald Baillie, *God was in Christ* (London, Faber, 1948), p. 58.
18. *Supra*, p. 18.
19. Mark 1: 22.
20. John 7: 46.

21. Luke 5: 8.
22. John 18: 6.
23. For an important discussion of this question, cf. Ninian Smart, 'Towards a Systematic Future for Theology', in *Prospect for Theology*, ed. F. G. Healey (London, Nisbet, 1966), pp. 95–116.
24. Quoted by David L. Edwards, *Religion and Change*, p. 353.
25. R. W. Dale, *The Atonement* (London, Congregational Union, 14th ed., 1892), p. 4.
26. 2 Cor. 5: 17.
27. Herbert McCabe, *Law, Love and Language*, p. 129.
28. 1 Cor. 10: 11.
29. Lionel Thornton, *The Common Life in the Body of Christ* (London, Dacre Press, 1944), p. 334.
30. C. S. Lewis, *The Pilgrim's Regress* (London, Bles, 1933), pp. 172 f.
31. 1 Cor. 15: 19.
32. Heb. 2: 8–9.
33. McCabe, op. cit., p. 134.
34. 2 Cor. 6: 2.

Acknowledgments

The author and publisher wish to acknowledge their indebtedness for permission to reproduce copyright material as follows: from *Areas of Ecumenical Experiment* by R. M. C. Jeffery, published by the British Council of Churches, London, 1968; from *Cathedrals in Modern Life*, published by the Church Information Office, London, 1961; from *New Christian*, article by William McSweeney in the issue of 8 August 1968.

Index